PRESENT MOMENT PARENTING

THE GUIDE TO A PEACEFUL LIFE WITH YOUR INTENSE CHILD

PRESENT MOMENT PARENTING

THE GUIDE TO A PEACEFUL LIFE WITH YOUR INTENSE CHILD

TINA FEIGAL, M.S. ED.

Parent and Teacher Coach

With a forward and contributions by

AMELIA FRANCK MEYER, MS, MSW, APSW, LISW

and

MECHELE PITT, MSSW, LICSW, LCSW

www.parentingmojo.com

Edited by Alicia Ester

ISBN 13: 978-1-59298-821-1
Library of Congress Control Number: 2017901525

Printed in the United States of America
First Printing: 2007
Revised Edition: 2017
21 20 19 18 17 5 4 3 2 1

Book design by Athena Currier

Beaver's Pond Press, Inc.
7108 Ohms Lane
Edina, MN 55439–2129

(952) 829-8818
www.BeaversPondPress.com

To order, visit www.ItascaBooks.com or call 1-800-901-3480 ext. 118. Reseller discounts available.

FOREWORD

When my children were young, we underwent a home remodeling project that was the result of water damage on all three levels of our house. Consequently, we all had to sleep on the top floor, then on the middle floor, then in the basement, and eventually at my mother-in-law's house and a hotel, while nearly all of our floors and ceilings were being replaced. During this period of transition, my two toddlers—twelve months and five days apart in age—had a very challenging time getting to and staying asleep.

I lamented to a colleague that I was so sleep deprived I could hardly function, and was ready to pay anyone to help me get a good night's sleep. My colleague said, "I know a miracle worker who can help you with your children." Never mind that I had two master's degrees in this subject area (a master's in social work and a master's in sociology/marriage and family), or that I had taught child development at the college level; I was still struggling mightily with this aspect of parenting. I had talked to everyone I knew, brought forward all of my old tricks from my days working in group homes with children, used Google for advice, and even instilled a "Bedtime Boot Camp" routine to try to get our family some rest, all to no avail—and then I met Tina Feigal.

After one meeting with Tina, my skeptical engineer husband said, "I think what she's teaching us is profound, and I think I could use it on you, too." After four sessions, I was sold! We were all sleeping again, and we were using Present Moment Parenting to bring harmony and peace to our home. I told Tina what I did for a living—at the time I was a CEO of a child welfare agency—and I knew that if I, with all of my background and training, needed this kind of parent coaching and support, so did other parents. We began working together shortly after that and have brought this life-changing model to all sorts of parents: bio, foster, step, adoptive, and single parents, and family members who are parenting kin.

During our time working together, we have refined this model to be trauma-informed and have applied these advanced parenting techniques to help all children, whether gifted and talented, struggling with behavioral concerns, recovering from trauma, diagnosed with autism, or any other childhood challenge. *Present Moment Parenting* works! The techniques you learn in this book will build a stronger connection between you and your child, will help to heal past hurts, and will build the strengths-based support needed for both you and your child to *thrive!* You will know that you've "got it" when the expression of love and affection from your child comes back to you in abundance! Happy parenting; remember, the days may seem long, but the years will seem short. Enjoy the journey!

—Amelia Franck Meyer, MS, MSW, APSW, LISW, CEO of Alia (www.aliainnovations.org)

CONTENTS

INTRODUCTION

The first edition of this book was released in 2007, and now it's time to add what we've discovered in the interim. Filled with powerful present moments, these years have informed my parent coaching work in a way that compels me to share new thoughts with you, while keeping the old ones that are "tried and true." I hope you enjoy this second edition, and that you not only read it, but make a commitment to using its contents toward a dramatically improved life for you and your entire family.

This book is updated to include information on the Ten Tenets of Present Moment Parenting; the effects of trauma on the brain of an abused or neglected child and what to do about them; mindfulness, self-compassion, and healthy vulnerability for parents. It's meant to be a resource for today's parenting, and our hope is that you read every page, and come away with "what to do" to improve your relationship with your child.

SETTING THE SCENE

Sarah is on the phone, describing her plight with her nine-year-old. "I am at the end of my rope. My daughter is headed for danger if this behavior keeps up. I've tried everything I know to get her to comply, but nothing works! She is defiant at every turn, and last night she got physical with me when I told her she couldn't bake cookies at 9:00 p.m. She was hitting, pulling my hair, kicking, and trying to bite me. I'm starting to feel afraid of my own child!"

If you're the parent of an intense child, you likely find that the traditional discipline techniques simply haven't worked. Repeating yourself (nicely and not-so-nicely), making your voice louder, adding emotion to your interactions, forcing your child to his or her room, grounding, taking away electronic devices, and restricting other freedoms have actually made the situation worse. Every time you try a new tactic, your child raises the bar and exceeds your level of intensity.

With this book, you will learn how to gain your child's cooperation using proven techniques that avoid the well-known pitfalls.

Renowned physician and psychotherapist Alfred Adler and, more recently, Barbara Fredrickson in her book *Positivity*, have brought forth the concept that providing emotional energy when things are going well is much more effective in improving behavior than increasing emotion when things are not going well, which is most parents' usual response. Using *Present Moment Parenting*, you will learn to replace your intense reaction to unwanted behavior with calmness, putting yourself in proactive mode. Your child's behavior will reflect your new approach in a surprisingly positive way. You will also learn to employ the incredible power of the present moment, which, when one considers it, is all we really have. The past is gone, and the future is not yet here. We really don't have power over either of them. Present Moment Parenting focuses your attention, not on using past experiences to predict future ones, but on harnessing the incredible power of this very moment to influence future moments.

You'll be measuring the helpfulness of each tip in the book based on the developmental stage of your child. The book is written for children of all ages, with trust in the reader to adjust the tips to specific situations. It wouldn't be practical to try to write the tips for each and every age group, but they are written for ease of adaptation, with the hope that parents and caregivers are able to gain from them no matter the age of the child.

This book is written with caring and support for parents, caregivers, grandparents, and all who love and care for children whose behavior can best be described as "intense." They are children of all ages, who may have diagnoses such as attention deficit hyperactivity disorder (ADHD), autism, oppositional defiant disorder (ODD), anxiety, attachment disorder, obsessive-compulsive disorder (OCD), gifted and talented, or any other of a variety of conditions. Or they may not have a diagnosis, but they're going through an adjustment, which just makes them hard to handle. The techniques included here apply to every child, so your intense one won't feel singled out. And new in this edition is a section on children who have experienced trauma. These kids need a specialized approach, as we now know that trauma at any age can cause *changes in the brain* that affect emotional and behavioral functioning. When it happens to children, their caregivers need the insights and compassion to weather the storms, and methods for healing the incredible hurts produced by neglect and abuse.

As a parent, grandparent, parent coach, and trainer of coaches, I offer you this book with hope, the real hope I regularly see on the faces and hear in the voices of my caring, loving, newly empowered clients and the clients of those whom I have certified to do this work. My dream for every parent who wants a coach to find one gets a step closer every day, and for that I am eternally grateful.

CHAPTER ONE

The Overview—Where Does Intense Behavior Come From?

Blake: major "fast" brain
"Ferrari sitting in traffic"—Dr. Jones

UNDERSTANDING THE CHILD'S BRAIN

The brain of an intense child is as intense as the behavior. If we could see into the child's brain using a Functional Magnetic Resonance Imaging (fMRI) scan, we would note that the activity within the brain is often less organized, faster, and more intense than that of the average brain. This is helpful to know, as we can now work with this information to create a situation that improves the troublesome behavior.

This intense brain is looking for a connection, just as we do when we fall in love or meet a new friend. Our brains, designed for survival, help us recognize "alikeness." We see reflections of ourselves in similar people and are drawn to them. We want to spend as much time as we can with them. When we do, our brains are experiencing highly rewarding connections at subconscious levels. Our togetherness is strongly reinforced, and we are compelled to repeat it.

A similar thing happens within the intense child's brain. But rather than a romantic connection, the child's brain is looking for an intensity connection, attempting to make the outer environment's level of intensity the same as the interior brain's level of intensity. The child seeks to stir things up, creating emotional explosions all around her. The brain is hungry for this connection, and that is why it appears that she seeks negative attention. No child really seeks negativity from the adults in her world. This connection urge is something the child is not consciously sensing, a fact that frees us from blaming the child for negative behavior. (We all know from experience how effective blaming and punishing are—not so much.) Whenever the intensity from the external environment connects with the intensity of the internal environment (brain), a reward occurs, and the behavior is likely to be repeated.

Another helpful field regarding brains and communication is that of "mirror neurons" in which we learn that if one person smiles, the other is wired to also smile. If one person yells, the other is also wired to yell. The mirror neurons keep us connected to others as a survival mechanism. Empathy is felt, we see ourselves in other humans, and the bond is strengthened. We cannot function on our own, and the body's wisdom is designed to keep us connected.

This general tendency toward intensity connections isn't unique to intense children. We are all looking for them. If you are a calm person, you want a calm exterior environment to connect with your calm interior environment. And if you're a high-intensity adult, you want more action. So how do we put a stop to the string of emotional explosions from children? We make the intensity connections occur when things are going well, rather than when an infraction has just occurred. Instead of rewarding negative behavior, we want to reward the positive behavior in *this present moment.* Whatever we want to see more of should get our intense attention. In other words, water the flowers, not the weeds.

For all children, connections to their parents or primary caregivers are key to their healthy emotional development. When a newborn looks up to her caregiver, and sees someone she can count on for food, shelter, clothing, communication, and loving touch, her neural pathways for trust develop nicely. If she looks up to her caregivers, and they do not, for whatever reason, provide the nurturing necessary, the child is forced to fill in the blanks in order to survive. Living in a world without a trusted caregiver causes the child's focus to turn to the self for nurture, and destroys the child's ability to trust adults. It also produces a storm of "see me" behaviors, as the organism child *knows* that caregiving is necessary to her survival. When adequate caregiving doesn't occur, the child's body has no choice but to try to get the attention of the caregiver. So when we see acting-out behavior, we need to look at unfulfilled needs, rather than trying to change the child. The need could be physical or emotional, and is often the latter. Whenever a child is not feeling seen for her true emotional state, she acts out from an unconscious place in her being, seeking to be seen, which assures her survival. When she's seen, she can relax, and the acting-out behavior loses its purpose. For expansion on this topic as it relates to children who have experienced trauma, see Chapter Six on Trauma-Effective Parenting.

WHY DOESN'T PUNISHMENT WORK?

Both personal experience and Psychology 101 tell us that punishment doesn't work. If you find yourself repeatedly punishing a child for the same behavior, your efforts are not working and it's time to try something new. Punishment does three things. First, it brings adults temporary relief from negative behavior. However, we are not looking for temporary, but a more permanent resolution. The second effect of punishment is that it creates a perceived need for retaliation. The child may not retaliate immediately, but may save up the payback for an unexpected time. This is when we often see negative behavior or tantrums "out of the blue." Again, the child is not seeking to be bad, but the brain keeps a scorecard of intensity, which appears to require equilibrium. Whenever the child is punished, a little marker gets left inside his head and heart, compelling him to respond by making the score even. This is, again, unconscious on the child's part. The third effect of punishment is creating fear. However, most parents would rather base their relationships with their children on love and support than on fear. Punishing just doesn't get us what we want: that warm, loving, cooperative relationship.

Cast blame aside and just see the child as an organism responding to his environment and need for survival. Work to leave a marker of triumph in his heart and brain whenever possible, encouraging messages like: "I am a good kid," "I can please these people," or "I can do the right thing." A child with these internal affirmations does not need to look for intensity around negativity. The intensity is around the good behaviors, so the brain will seek its connection there. You'll then see more positive behavior!

NO GUILT

It is utterly understandable if you have been punishing your child's negative behavior up to this point. It may have been the only tool you had in your tool bag to stop negative behavior. Many of us were raised with this perspective, and in fact, much of our society is based upon looking for infractions and punishing for them. However, this is not effective with intense children and, in fact, punishment makes the behavior worse. Its other effect is to set the child on a journey of progressively limited freedoms that starts at home with small behavior restrictions, and continues at school with detention, then suspension, and possibly expulsion and school failure. The natural sequence of these events leads too many children to the juvenile justice system, and eventually adult detention and prison. We can stop this self-perpetuating cycle by intervening now, using the present moment to help the child form a whole new self-image that leads her to affirm, "I am successful and worthy of positive feedback."

THE CHILD AS AN ORGANISM: UNDERSTANDING THE EFFECT OF YOUR INPUT ON HIS HEART

At the Institute of HeartMath (IHM), researchers discovered a very helpful finding: the heart is responsive to emotional input. This is something we see in poetry and love songs, but now scientists can see that the rhythm of the heartbeat changes when positive emotion is infused into the heart. When we receive any emotionally charged message, positive or negative, we actually have an emotion-generated physiological effect, not unlike blushing. Connecting with a child using a positive comment causes a similar reaction. Maybe you've noticed what a child looks like when you really "hit home" with a compliment or affirmation. You might say something like, "When you were speaking so politely to Ms. Harrison at school yesterday, it just made me feel *so* proud of you!" The child's eyes turn downward, he tries not to smile, and he maybe even gets a little teary. Or maybe he beams from ear to ear. Those are physiological responses!

Another IHM discovery is that the heart has its own neurological system that sends messages to the brain. So as mentioned earlier, when we give children our input, we create and strengthen the heart-to-brain neural pathway that says, "I am a good kid. I can do the right thing. I can please my parents and teacher. I am successful." Alternatively, our input can also deliver the heart-brain message, "I am not a good kid. I can never do the right thing. I can't please my parents and teacher. I am a failure." We have a choice about what to infuse into the child. It's our job as adults to shape the future by using this moment to give his heart the sustenance it needs to grow and become the heart it was meant to be. The child is an organism, just like a plant. If we put the plant in sunlight and give it water and fertilizer, it grows to become the plant it was intended to be. If we put it in a closet and shut the door, it withers, turns brown, and dies. If we deliver negative messages to a child, he will turn sour and become anxious, depressed, and oppositional. If we deliver the sunshine of heartfelt appreciation, the rain of clarity, and the nutrients of values shared when there is no infraction, the organism will grow and blossom into the child he was destined to be.

THE TEN TENETS OF PRESENT MOMENT PARENTING

1. Attunement in the present moment is vital for a healthy parent-child relationship.

"Attunement" is defined as the feeling of being "at one" with another human being. Or you might think in terms of musical instruments, tuning to one another with increasingly close sounds until they match. With parenting, attunement means joining the child where she is in the present moment. Not judging, not fixing, but just joining. It is remarkable how therapeutic it is for the child when parents do this. And it's also remarkable that once attuned to, the child's behavior improves and the relationship with her parents is strengthened.

Example: Your eleven-year-old is having an all-out tantrum because she had her heart set on sleeping over at a friend's house, and now the plans have to change due to a family emergency. She screams, cries, slams, swears, and throws things around her room. After you wait out the storm, you go to her and say, "That was such a disappointment to miss sleeping at Ava's. I really see it." Then stop. Just let the silence work its magic for several minutes. You have expressed to the child that you "see her," which was the purpose of her wild behavior. Keep this in mind: all misbehavior is a readable signal, a call for *being seen.*

Then say, "I'll be downstairs and *as soon as you*" (great words to predict the positive future) "get this cleaned up, let's call Ava and make a plan for next time." You haven't ignored that she threw everything in her room; you've let her know you expect her to clean it up; and you have "forwarded the action" to restore her hope. More important, you have not yelled, accused, demanded, or commanded, all of which would have resulted in a bigger blowout than ever, and a wounded parent-child relationship. When you come together again, it would not be surprising to hear an apology from your daughter, as you've left the door open for one. Or you may just see a softening or increase in affection. That's how you know you've hit the "sweet spot" of seeing your child in the present moment, and assuring her that she's emotionally safe in your care. If you had come on strong, she would have needed to defend herself, likely for days, with sullenness or the silent treatment. But instead, you have kept your cool when she lost hers. That's what parents need to do to help their children gain self-control. Being the "adult" to your child's "child" is enormously challenging, but the rewards are incredible.

2. The overarching goal of every child is to feel lovable.

When your child acts the least lovable, that's the time to realize he needs love the most. You may ask, "Isn't that spoiling him?" or "Doesn't he need to be taught how to behave?" No, and yes. When he's out of control, he's letting you know that he's not able to pull himself together. But he still needs connection and love, now more than ever. He's a child, after all, and emotional regulation is a learned process. Ask yourself if your response is supportive of his process, or if it interferes by making him feel guilty for strong emotion. Childhood is filled with strong emotion, and you're better off anticipating it as normal versus finding it unacceptable.

Example: Your nine-year-old son is playing video games and you've told him three times that it's time to stop. He has a major fit when you finally approach him to turn off the computer. He says,

"It's not fair! I was in the middle of that level! You can't do this to me!" He gives the chair a shove and it careens off the wall, leaving a dent. He stomps to his room, slams the door, and yells, "I hate you!" at the top of his lungs. And yes, despite all this drama, he needs love now. Your gut tells you to go into his room and give him a piece of your mind, starting with, "Listen, young man . . . " But if you stop and take a few breaths to remember the basic tenet that every child needs to feel lovable, you can use this negative experience as an opportunity to teach love instead of retaliation. Remember that what you do teaches your child much more powerfully than what you say.

Let him calm down, and then approach him with, "It was really hard for you to stop the game tonight, wasn't it?" "Yes, you made me stop and I won't be able to find my place again! And I had my best score ever!" "You're really mad at me for that." "Yes, I am!" "Do you understand why I needed you to get off the game right then?" "Yes, my time was up." "Good, I'm glad you realize that when we set a rule, it sticks." "I'm sorry." "I know you are. Let's set it up so this doesn't happen again." "OK."

Then meet as a family (more on this in Chapter Two, Day Three) to decide together how time on video games should be handled. If you include your child in the solution in advance, you are much more likely to see cooperation instead of defiance. Discuss options, write them down, consider what your child says very carefully, and ask for clarity. After your decision is made, i.e., "We will have a timer on the computer and it will simply turn off at the designated time. The player will need to plan playing time accordingly," you can show your appreciation for your child engaging in the dialogue. Yes, it takes time to do this, but it's time worth spending up front, so that you're not reacting to negative behavior on the back end. The "return on investment" of your time and consideration is invaluable.

Note: Keep in mind that your child may have a "more compelling reason" or MCR for playing the game than for complying with your request to get off. It's your job to provide an MCR for getting off the video game. In days past, punishment or threat of punishment was the MCR. Today, we know that other MCRs work better. In fact, leading your child to his higher self through cooperation is the MCR, as nothing can compare with the experience of the heart telling the brain, "I am a good kid." So this is where heartfelt appreciation comes in, to build the child's sense of self. "When you get off the game at the time we decided on, I feel so impressed and relieved. It shows me that our peaceful relationship really means something to you."

3. With every interaction, parents are either pushing their children away or drawing them near.

You might want to focus on this tenet for a few days, and just watch how your child responds, verbally and non-verbally, to your approach. Are you pushing her away or drawing her near? After you become more aware of this dynamic, you'll be able to adjust your interactions to more drawing near. Watch how your child responds to "being seen" and "feeling felt" by you. You'll notice an almost instant increase in communication and cooperation. It's actually surprising how easy this is.

Drawing near statements:

> *"Thanks for helping with the groceries today. You lighten my load, and I'm so grateful."*
>
> *"Did you notice how those people in the restaurant were acting? What did you think of that?"*
>
> *"When your little brother approached you with a question, you just answered it for him. I loved seeing that. Did you know he really looks up to you, even though he can't always say so?"*
>
> *"I need your help with this problem, and I value your opinion very much."*
>
> *"Are you the one who left that room so clean last evening? Thank you!"*
>
> *"I can't get over how many things we do every day. Do you sometimes want a break, too? Let's just rest on Saturday and do whatever we want."*
>
> *"Take your time." (Consider how infrequently children in today's world hear this phrase. It's usually, "Hurry, hurry, hurry!")*

4. Staying in the present moment reduces parents' fear of past or future behaviors.

The present is all you have, so use it to your best advantage. Eckhart Tolle, author of *The Power of Now* and *A New Earth,* points out that nothing has ever happened in the past, and nothing will ever happen in the future. Everything happens in the present moment. Make this very moment with the child in front of you the best it can be by responding in a positive way. String a bunch of these present moments together, and the future will take care of itself. Releasing previous scenarios will open the space to create new ones; your interactions with your child will all be aimed at the goal of turning negative behavior around, not digging up the past. Only "teaching attention" (in the form of do-overs, which we'll get into more later in the chapter) goes to him when things are going poorly, but copious positive attention flows to him when rules are not being broken, and when behavior is appreciated.

5. All behavior is a readable signal.

Yesterday I spoke with a woman who was telling me that a six-year-old boy was suddenly using a lot of sexual and potty language, and he'd even smeared feces in the bathroom for the first time in his life. As awful as this image is, I encouraged her not to focus on the behavior, but instead, on what was being communicated by the child. My educated guess is that he's been traumatized, and that an investigation should take place. Do not ever hesitate to report abuse if you see a child suddenly communicating that something is terribly wrong. The communication is not direct, as children lack the tools to clearly state what happened, so we need to get good at "reading" the behavior, looking for the meaning behind it, rather than responding to it as "inappropriate," "disrespectful," or "immature."

And sometimes, behavioral signals are milder. You may see a formerly bouncy, happy child become sad. Get to the root of the behavior by saying, "I see you're quieter than before. I'm wondering what's up. Let's go for a walk and you can tell me." (Note: Kids find it much easier to talk if they're riding in the car or walking. There's less pressure than if you're sitting across from them, just waiting for a response.)

6. Respectfully addressing the child's true feelings eliminates the need for punishment.

If you feel like a child needs a punishment, try this instead:

> *"I see that you just said some harsh words to your mom that she really didn't deserve. I think that's because you're having some big stress right now. I don't think you meant to be disrespectful. Want to tell me what's causing you to feel upset?"*
>
> *"I don't know."*
>
> *"If I guess, will you tell me if I'm right or wrong?"*

Be willing to be wrong. When you guess correctly, you'll relieve the stress of that huge feeling in your child. When you guess incorrectly, you'll hear the correction. Then without judgment, say, "Thank you for telling me. It's helpful when I know your strong feelings, and we can deal with them respectfully." Then leave the space open for your child to apologize to Mom for the harsh words. You'll be surprised how willing she is to say she's sorry when no one forces her to do it. Give heartfelt appreciation for her sharing, and for the apology.

7. The child's body is affected by emotional input from the parent.

Your child is living in a body that responds to what is said to him. The response is either receptive or rejecting, and you as the parent have the choice to build the receptive responses by being aware that your child's body is always responding. The amygdala, near the brain stem, senses a threat to your child when harsh words are spoken. If you are in the habit of ordering your child to do things, or threatening consequences, you are triggering the amygdala and the response will be one of rejection, every single time. Just knowing this one thing can help you elicit much more open and receptive responses from your child. If your usual requests look like this: "Get those dishes to the dishwasher and start that reading assignment so you don't get in trouble at school tomorrow," you are triggering the rejection response. Instead, respectfully addressing your child with, "As soon as you get your dishes to the dishwasher, I'm ready to review that reading assignment with you," will allow the receptive parts of your child's brain to be activated.

8. The greatest human need is to be needed.

Three thousand years from now, when archaeologists dig up our society, what will they find, and what conclusions will they draw from those findings? They will find iPads, iPods, DSs, DVRs, TVs, computers, movie theaters, and stadiums. Their natural conclusion will be that we were a society that needed to be entertained. This is all well and good, except that it completely misses the incredibly vital point that the greatest human need is to be needed. We do our children a huge disservice by taking care of all the adult needs of family life while they play video games or watch TV. We fail to prepare them for the fabulous feeling of being useful to others, which cannot and should not be overlooked. The glue that sticks humanity together is helping one another, and when children don't grow up being helpful, they miss the very thing we're wired to do in order to survive as a society. So get a little lazy, allow your children to be helpful, and show your appreciation, not every time, but every fifth time. That way they will avoid becoming "praise junkies," only wanting to help if there's a reward of compliments. They'll also feel, with appropriately sprinkled appreciation, as if their assistance is truly needed. This is how you help a child form true self-esteem. By the way, it's the *only* way to help a child form true self-esteem.

9. The parents' role is to support and guide their children as they become capable in their own right.

You've heard the term "helicopter parent" way too many times in recent media posts. Have you wondered if you might be one? A helicopter parent hovers over the child, assuming the role of protector, with the best of intentions. He or she will overly monitor the activities of the child, and consistently step in to correct any flaws or situations that seem detrimental to the child. These good intentions are often misguided, as children *need to learn for themselves.* When we overprotect our toddlers, grade-schoolers, middle-schoolers, and teens, we rob them of the experience of self-efficacy (figuring it out for myself, and finding my own solutions). The importance of allowing this self-directedness cannot be overstated. Employers and colleges nationwide have seen an enormous uptick in students and new employees who cannot fend for themselves, on even the most basic tasks of life.

Will you know it if you start to do too much for your child? Here are some ways you can tell:

a. Every time your young child falls or bumps, you ask, "Are you OK?" instead of waiting for the child to let you know whether she's OK. This actually robs the child of self-comforting skills, which are vital to her development.

b. When a situation arises that may displease your child, you try hard to think of ways to ease the pain. This is normal for parents, but please note that it can be way overdone. Allowing some emotional distress into your child's life teaches him to handle it on his own. If you are constantly "sweeping in front of your child," he won't develop coping skills. Allow the distress, watch and wait to see how he handles it first, and then step in if he seems overwhelmed. Rather than providing a fix, provide reflection. "That was hard for you to accept. I see that you're calming yourself down now. You're getting good at that!"

c. You feel tempted to do, or be overly involved, in homework. Of course you want your child to be successful in school. Every parent does! But if the success comes from you instead of from her, is it really success? Do everything you can to let your child's school life be her school life, as small successes, and especially small failures, are the best teachers. If you raise a child who doesn't know how to correct a small failure because you're not allowing them to happen, you are interfering with her learning. Let it go, let the teacher provide the correction, and let your child learn not only content, but self-correction.

d. You want to advocate for your child with teachers, coaches, and instructors of all types, so he has the best experience possible. Again, this is normal. But beware of "maximizing" every experience your child has, as it communicates the message "Unless it's perfect, life is not acceptable." A small amount of heads-up to the coach or teacher is just fine, but apply the "wait and watch" habit here, as well. If you let your child go to third grade or soccer practice with a clean slate, he may just surprise you with abilities you didn't know he had, which could render your warning to the coach or teacher unnecessary. Each year, children grow and develop, which is something you can count on. Wait and watch what he does, and then wait and watch some more. Try to focus on successes, and don't interfere with his relationship with his team, his class, or his mentors. It's his job to navigate this territory, and if you need to step in, you'll know. There will be ongoing distress that he can't overcome, which is your invitation to offer an insight to the mentor. Otherwise, encourage him to communicate his needs directly. If he's too young, and you see that insurmountable distress, offer what you know, and then back away again.

10. Parents do the best they can with the tools they have.

In our work as parent coaches, we are always mindful that parents are truly doing their best. They may be tapping something they read or heard in a parenting class, or they may be doing what their parents did. If it's not working, there's work to be done, but coaches are not in the business of judging parents. Support, understanding, and new parenting ideas are the only helpful components of coaching, so that's what parents experience during sessions.

THE NEW WAY

Our strategy now changes from giving emotional intensity (demonstrated by wide eyes, loud or angrily soft voices, and big gestures) for unwanted behavior, to delivering emotional rewards for desired behavior. This seems simple enough, but its practical application has its challenges. As adults, we are so programmed to respond to negative behavior in order to teach children lessons that we need to exert significant effort to put our emphasis elsewhere. The good thing about emphasizing the positive is that it really works. Not only will it dramatically improve your child's behavior, but it's also so rewarding to you personally that your sense of yourself as a parent will take a huge leap forward.

Tip: If you wouldn't speak in the tone of voice you're using to an adult friend, don't do it with your child.

CREATING THE INTENSITY CONNECTION AROUND THE "GOOD STUFF"

Whenever something goes right, add intensity to your positive comment by saying, "When you _______ I feel _______ because _______." This becomes the positive equivalent of the old negativity or yelling, by creating a much more emotionally charged message than does the typical "thanks" or "good job." We are looking to infuse an incredible amount of positivity, creating an intensity connection for your child's brain. We want to cause a strong emotional reaction, just as yelling does, only on the positive side. Using "When you _______ I feel _______ because _______." serves the purpose well. We'll refer to it here as "heartfelt appreciation."

THE PARENT AS HEALER

Applying Present Moment Parenting to a child's challenging behaviors is the best way to bring about the healing you desire. This model employs the power of the relationship between you and your child, where love and connection already exist. Present Moment Parenting is perfect in that it can be woven into your child's life twenty-four hours a day, seven days a week, rather than for an hour a week, which happens with typical therapy sessions. Also, the intense child is often not likely to respond well to a therapist's questions about feelings and motivation. When the child answers a therapist's queries with "I don't know," she is telling the truth. She doesn't understand the workings of her intensity-hungry brain as it looks for a connection in the environment. But we as adults can help her brain locate where the intensity is and where it is not, and bring about the changes we desire for the child and for ourselves. Am I saying that traditional therapy never helps? No. But we have found that if a child is in therapy, Present Moment Parenting is a powerful adjunct that supports parents and helps kids get better. In the absence of therapy, or when a child refuses the therapy offered, Present Moment Parenting can still be highly effective.

Here are the results of our Pre- and Post-Coaching Questionnaires by parents:

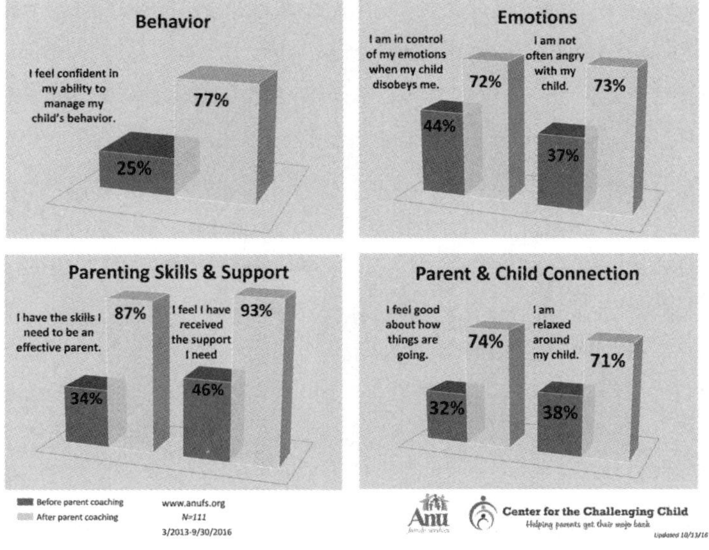

CONSISTENCY: THE SUPREME CHALLENGE

I often hear from parents that they have a hard time staying consistent with their children. They are tired, hurried, hassled, and worn out. They just want their child to behave, but the harder they try to gain cooperation, the worse the situation becomes. How does a parent stay with the child whose brain is seeking intensity without "losing it" on a regular basis? With Present Moment Parenting, it's easier to stay in what I call "the parent place" than you think. First, get your mind set in advance. Do a little mental run-through of the last altercation with your child. See yourself responding calmly, by *taking time to breathe together* with your child, and then a simple "Let's have a do-over." (See more on this later in this chapter.) Then visualize the next infraction. See yourself responding this way again. Remind yourself to let go of the past, with all of its tirades, tantrums, hurtful words, and negotiations, as it is over and cannot be changed.

Note: The definition of insanity is repeating the same thing over and over and expecting different results. If you have tried your old techniques many times with little or no improvement, it's time for a change. Also, take note of whether your child is repeating the behavior and expecting different results. Teach him not to do this. Employ direct teaching by rehearsing better responses to frustrating situations, so that he can grow in his social interactions by actually feeling his body and mind having an appropriate response.

EXERCISE:

Use this moment to check in with your child. Is there something occurring right now that you can reward with your heartfelt appreciation? Do it. Come back and record it here.

____

____

____

____

____

____

____

____

Consistency comes not from doling out strict discipline when things are going poorly, but from making a decision about your reaction in advance, and rehearsing the improved scene while there is no issue. When you have decided to stay in the parent place and never waver from your plan, half the battle is won. You can now remain solid in your position, and no amount of whining, threatening, arguing, throwing, bullying, swearing, or "I-hate-you"s will change it. You are certain that you will always give your child what she needs: heartfelt appreciation when things are going well, and a do-over when they are not. This is the most loving combination you can offer. You win because you have eliminated the guilt of inconsistency, while feeling secure in your stance. Your child wins because she knows what your responses will be. This creates the predictability and security she craves.

Please note that children crave a high intensity connection while at the same time they crave predictability and security. This is simply the nature of children. While they attempt to gain mastery over their interactions, parts of their development are not in sync with other parts. So yes, children often crave intensity, and also need a great deal of security to help them learn appropriate responses. Think of predictability as the stage upon which they develop their skills, and intensity connections for good behavior as the acting method you are teaching.

All of this translates into a deep love that transforms the former state of upheaval and anxiety. Your daily life with your child can now be much more enjoyable, calm, and serene. Surely there will be some backsliding, and certainly you'll see some testing, but your consistent response, based on your predetermined reaction to unwanted behavior, will bring things back into focus very quickly. Staying in the parent place is now your preferred way of being, reinforced every day by the improvements you see in your child.

WHEN SHOULD I TEACH MY VALUES?

As parents we usually try to impart our values at the time when the child is least receptive: when the child misbehaves. We can lecture all we want at this time, but the child doesn't absorb one bit of the message. The emotions are running too high, and the words just don't sink in.

The best time to teach values is when things are going well. Use the dinner table, travel time, tuck-in time, videos, TV, relationship issues (your daily life with bosses, co-workers, and relatives), and all the regular incidents of life, as occasions to share your values. Even if what happened in life or what was on TV conflicts with your values, grab the opportunity to critique it to teach your child what you want him to know now, while you have him in the learning laboratory of your family. Time is precious, and kids grow up so fast. So many lessons need to be learned, and although you may not always feel it, your time together is limited. Use your present moment.

Here's an example: when your child looks about to engage in a full-blown tantrum or attack, you can avert it. Use the present moment to rejoice about the fact that he hasn't said any bad words, even if you think he would have in the next moment. Seek every opportunity to infuse a positive message into your child's mind and heart, even if you have to fudge a bit. It's worth your time and effort, and it helps him realize he is doing the right thing and being triumphant, even if just for a millisecond. When you intervene with positive messages, you maximize the present and begin to build a foundation of accomplishments. This can, again, be thought of as building a "string of successes" from which you can encourage more successes. From there, you can use present moments to talk about past successes, continuing to reinforce what you want by teaching your values here and now.

EXERCISE:

Write three of your family's values. Examples are: honesty, good manners, and respectful language.

1. ______________________________

2. ______________________________

3. ______________________________

Describe how you most recently communicated these three values to your child(ren). Note whether you did this at the time of an infraction, or when things were calm.

1. The value: ________________________________
How I communicated it: ___________________________
____

When I communicated:
______After the infraction
______When things were calm

2. The value: ________________________________
How I communicated it: ___________________________
____

When I communicated:
______After the infraction
______When things were calm

3. The value: ________________________________
How I communicated it: ___________________________
____

When I communicated:
______After the infraction
______When things were calm

Now make a plan for sharing your three values at the best possible time, when things are going well. Think about using the present moment to your best advantage. Use TV, travel time, movies, or life experiences as the context for a constructive, enjoyable conversation. These may be from yesterday or last week.

Definitely feel free to discuss them after the fact, as mentioned above, to strengthen the teaching of your values. Write your plans on the space provided below:

1. ____

____

2. ____

____

3. ____

____

To help you get the conversation started, here are some phrases to use:

> *"I was just thinking of that time last week when my cousin Sara called to tell me about her son. Remember, he got into trouble at school? Let's talk about how we would handle his situation in our family."*

Note: Use of the phrase "in our family" is powerful in its ability to create and expand your family identity. This fulfills a need that is basic to every human being: belongingness (from Abraham Maslow's hierarchy of needs.) Use "in our family" whenever you can. "In our family, we treat each other with respect and kindness, and you are part of our family." These are powerful inclusion words that foster and anchor belongingness in the child.

> *"You were so wonderful yesterday when Taylor called to ask you over to his house. You told him you had to check with me, which I really appreciate. You are really learning how to get what you need in such a respectful way!"*

With this comment you have:

- Shown your heartfelt appreciation with a "When you _______, I feel _______ because _______" statement
- Taught your value (obeying the "ask permission" rule) directly
- Infused a ton of positivity into your child's heart, sending the heart-to-brain message, "I am a good kid. I can do the right thing."
- Increased the likelihood that it, or something equally positive, will happen again

"When you fed the dog this morning, I was thinking about how she depends on you for so much—you play with her, you let her out, you throw the ball with her, and you feed her! What would that dog do without you?"

With this comment, you have:

- Shared your values about taking care of a pet
- Shown your heartfelt appreciation
- Infused positivity into your child's heart
- Increased his sense of being a caretaker in a healthy way
- Increased the likelihood of this behavior, or something even better, occurring again

USING ROLE PLAY AND DO-OVERS TO TEACH BETTER BEHAVIOR

Another wonderful tool for bringing out the best in children is to role play troublesome situations. Let's say your child comes home with a story about how a kid on the bus took her hat and threw it. Your child got angry and went after the other kid, and was promptly reported to the principal for misbehaving on the bus. This is the third time it's happened, and you can see the handwriting on the wall: soon your child will be banned from the bus.

The best way to teach your child what you want her to know is to replay the scene, helping her come up with a response that does not get her into trouble. (This is a great stance to take: "I just don't want to see you getting into trouble anymore.") Decide who should be your child and who should be the other kid. Set up some chairs to represent the bus. Rehearse the scene exactly as she said it happened, disregarding whether it is absolutely "true." The important thing is her perception of the scene, as this is what is true for her. Replay the scene with a better response, such as ignoring the kid who threw the hat, and asking for the hat as you leave the bus. Then trade roles, so your child can be in the other child's shoes, too, which broadens her perspective on the scene. (This is especially good for kids who need help developing empathy.)

Role playing every scene you want to see improved is a powerful way to "build a map in the child's brain" for the way things can occur. Being young, kids often don't realize they have alternatives to fighting back or lashing out when someone annoys them. Role playing gives them that alternative in a very real way. It only takes a few moments, and is a powerful method for teaching the child's body a new response to conflict. It's also fun! If the child doesn't understand the alternative response right away, just repeat the role playing until it sinks in.

As stated above, an additional tool for bringing out the best in kids is the "do-over." If your child whines, for example, you can take a few breaths together, and then ask for a do-over so that she can learn to speak in a tone that your ears can accept. Rehearse this at a time when there is no infraction, so that the learning can readily occur.

> You: Let's figure out how to get rid of some of the whining in this house. You know how I'm always saying, 'No whining'?

Your child will be relieved you're aware that you're often correcting her about this.

> You: I'll whine and you say 'do-over,' and then I'll ask for what I want in a better tone of voice. 'Moooommmm, can I go over to Emily's . . . pleeeeeeeease? Moooommmm, I said I want to go to Emileeeee's. Listen to meeeeeee.
>
> Child: "Do-over!"
>
> You (in a normal tone of voice): 'Mom, is it OK if I go to Emily's?'

This teaches the child to state things in a tone to which others can respond without feeling frustrated. Then switch roles, so that your child can learn from both perspectives how the exchange should sound.

And be sure that, when your child later uses a tone you can accept, you respond to her as quickly as possible with heartfelt appreciation. "I love that tone of voice, Honey. It shows me that you really know how to get a person's attention!" You have now assured yourself of less whining, and you've both had fun creating a new way of doing things!

EXERCISE:

On the next page describe a recent incident in which you let your own needs go while attempting to restore peace, or correct your child's impulsive negative behavior.

Example: You gave in to your child and bought something for him that you thought was extravagant. Your values were interfered with, and it was a hit to your sense of yourself as a competent money manager.

Now imagine that you had applied the principles of "placing the mask over your own mouth first." Give your child the loving, predictable consequences he needs while maintaining your own composure and financial wisdom. Re-write the incident here.

MY PROGRESS NOTES

Obstacles to implementing the ideas in this chapter:

Ways I will overcome the obstacles:

After using the ideas in this chapter, here's my success story:

CHAPTER TWO

Your Two-Week Guide to a Dramatically Improved Life with Your Intense Child

Here is a day-by-day schedule that you can follow while learning to employ Present Moment Parenting.

Use it strictly as a guide. If your Day One lasts a week, so be it. The important thing is to give yourself time to adjust your interactions with your challenging child at your perfect pace. Trust your instincts.

DAY ONE—GET YOUR MIND READY

Prepare yourself mentally to help your child change her behavior by just starting to notice your child's tiny victories. This is more effective than simply catching kids being good. Recognize what is going right in the ordinary present moments. Do not say anything yet; just notice.

DAY TWO—BEGIN TO INFUSE POSITIVITY

Take three or four opportunities today to give heartfelt appreciation to your child. Use the present moment to stop and take stock. Is there something happening right now that you appreciate? Is there a tiny moment of peace and quiet (remember, your brain is looking for an intensity connection, too, and the level it wants is "low!"). Is your child behaving in such a way that could even be remotely construed as positive, such as speaking in an indoor voice, keeping his hands to himself, or holding still? Even if it's happening for a nanosecond, take the opportunity to infuse positivity into your child's heart.

Use your three-part statement of heartfelt appreciation:

> *"When _______ I feel _______ because _______."*

For example:

> *"When you put your plate in the dishwasher, I was extremely proud of you because it shows me how grown up you are!"*
>
> *"When you played nicely with the baby, I was so touched. I can tell how sensitive you are to her needs."*
>
> *"When you spoke to my cousin on the phone just now, you were so polite, and just handed the phone right to me. Do you know what you did? You built a bridge between Janelle and me! Thank you so much!"*

Remember, these three-part statements are the emotional impact equivalent of yelling. They land more firmly in your child's mind and heart than do "Good job answering the phone," and "Thanks for putting your plate in the dishwasher." More examples of how to make heartfelt appreciation very effective follow.

INFUSING POWERFUL POSITIVITY BY INCLUDING FEELING LANGUAGE

When you . . .

- clean up
- tell me about your friends
- say "OK" when I ask you something
- go to bed when asked
- control your strong feelings
- put on your hat and coat
- surprise me by doing your chores
- help your brother with a game
- hang up your jacket
- share your toys
- start homework without being told

I feel . . .

- rested
- close to you
- relieved
- listened to
- my heart getting so big
- so excited
- important and loved
- respected
- appreciative
- proud
- cared about
- impressed

because . . .

- it helps Mom's day go better
- it makes us feel close to each other
- there's no screaming
- I don't have to ask more than once
- you worked hard to help us get along
- we get Sister to school on time
- I know you are trying to do well
- you are listening to my request
- we don't have to pick up after you
- I see the generous person you are
- we'll get to do other things together

Pat yourself on the back. You have started the physiological change in your child's body by infusing positivity into her heart. With repetition, the heart-to-brain neural pathway that says "I am a good kid" or "I'm sensitive to the needs of others" will be strengthened. And you will see that the behavior of the child who thinks of herself this way is dramatically improved. Eventually, you'll transition to "When you . . . *you must feel* . . . because . . . " to support the child's sense of self-directedness and personal accomplishment. This is what creates an emotionally healthy future adult.

DAY THREE—THE FAMILY MEETING AND RULES

Make a plan for a family meeting. Collaborate with your spouse or another trusted adult, or decide to do it on your own. Determine a time and day that works for you and your family members. Sunday evening at 6:00 p.m. is a common family meeting time. Plan to meet every week or more often if situations come up. Or you may just meet because you enjoy this process.

Each family member is free to call a meeting when he sees a need. It doesn't have to be a serious thing, and in fact, the lighter it is, the better it is for the kids. They'll respond much better to something that involves fun than to a heavy-feeling encounter. Let the meeting feel casual enough for their comfort. Say, "We'll need you to decide where we meet, what music we'll have in the background, who will light the candle and who will blow it out, and what we'll have for snacks."

Read the following in advance of holding the family meeting:

Organizations of all types, including churches, governments, companies, and clubs, meet to discuss their processes. I often wonder why the exception to this rule is the family, the most important unit of society, and the one upon which all societal success depends. It's time to institute regular family meetings so that families can be as strong as other organizations.

In keeping with the spirit of Present Moment Parenting, hold meetings to lift up the children by pointing out achievements of the whole family. And when there is an issue that needs the family's attention, use the resource of the wisdom of each family member to resolve it.

HOLDING A SUCCESSFUL FAMILY MEETING

1. **Invite the children to the meeting,** showing the same respect for them that you would for an adult. If the children aren't available due to homework, etc., ask for an alternative time. Buy-in increases when the children are respected and feel they have a voice in the process. If they don't want to come to the meeting, do not insist. Hold it anyway, and watch how they get pulled in by curiosity. They will eventually get used to meetings as the "family norm," especially when they realize that the meetings are pleasant and that the children will have a valuable voice in the process.

2. **State that the purpose of the meeting** is to decide together how things are going in the family, to share accomplishments, and to make improvements where necessary.

3a. **Use a talking piece,** a symbol that grants the person holding it the right to speak his or her mind without being interrupted. It should have some significance for the whole family. It could be a statue, a photo of all of you, or a memento from a family vacation. The family may even want to create a new talking piece as a shared activity. In some families, each child makes one, and their use is rotated each week.

3b. **Whoever has the talking piece speaks, and whoever doesn't have the talking piece listens.** Listening is such a vital component to living a successful adult life. It's amazing how little focus it receives and how little training we get in it. Use this opportunity to teach your children what you want them to know about listening. When you notice them listening, say, "I noticed you're listening very well! I bet you can even tell me what your brother just said." Then listen carefully as your child repeats what he heard, and follow with heartfelt appreciation for listening so well. "You did hear what your brother said! I knew you were a great listener!" You have just strengthened the "listener" identity of your child, and you will see good listening again.

3c. **The speaker continues speaking until completely finished,** rather than being rushed to finish so others can speak. (This takes the pressure to finish off the speaker, and removes the conflict over the talking piece. It also teaches others patience with the speaker. Allow plenty of time for the first meeting.)) Anyone can have the talking piece back when he has something else to say—all within reason, of course.

4. **If you have some issues with interrupting,** have one family member, on a rotating basis, take charge of making sure that the listeners listen while the speaker speaks. If the monitor is one of the children, be sure to deliver your heartfelt appreciation for a job well done.

5. **Devote the entire first meeting to what you love about being in the family,** and **then end the meeting.** This leaves the children with a positive feeling about being contributing members of the family and about participating in meetings. Start each meeting by saying what you love.

6. **At the second meeting,** start by having each person say what he or she loves about being in the family, and then bring up an issue you want resolved. Just describe what takes place without emotion, as if you are reporting the news.

   For example:

   "Every evening it seems we have a lot of arguing at bedtime. Here's what happens, and tell me if I am getting this right: I say, 'It's time for bed,' and you ignore me. Then my voice gets louder. I say, 'Let's get your pajamas on,' and you leave the room. My voice gets more irritated and I say, 'Time to brush your teeth.' You jump on the bed. I say, 'It's time to pick out a story,' and you run downstairs. My voice gets louder and louder and pretty soon I'm nagging you, and in a little while I'm yelling. I can tell you one thing: I hate to yell at you. And I'm pretty sure you hate being yelled at. Is that right?" The children will likely respond with a heartfelt "yes!" Continue with: "Let's do what we always do, which is that we always get pajamas on; we always brush teeth; we always read a story; and we always turn off the light, only without the nagging. Would you like that?" Again, the kids will likely feel relief, and offer an enthusiastic "yes!" If they give the slightest approval, or even if they don't, just compassionately continue with the meeting.

THE RULES

Then say, "OK, we're going to need a list of rules so we can help our family get along the very best we can. What should the rules be?" Having the kids make the rule list increases buy-in to the process. You can act as their secretary and write down what they say, which communicates even more of a feeling of importance to their contributing to the list. After they're finished with the list, add whatever rules you think still need to be included. Then point out that you as the parent reserve the right to make up rules on the spot whenever you see the need. That way, you won't get into a struggle about enforcing rules that aren't on the list. The rules should start with "no." This is most helpful for intense kids who often have auditory processing issues (ADHD, hyperfocus, giftedness, and other situations, as well). They hear the sounds just fine, but the storage, retrieval, and interpretation of the sounds is not the same as it is for other kids. That's why lengthy explanations are often lost on these kids. It's not that they are not listening, but their brains' processing keeps them from knowing what the sounds mean. So a very clear "no interrupting" or "no loud noises" is the best for helping them achieve success in following the rules.

How long should the list be? A list of five to seven rules works well. You'll need more if you have a wide age-range in your family, or perhaps you'll want a big kids' list and a little kids' list. The list is for the whole family, so parents follow the rules the same as the kids. Explain that the rule list will be revised as necessary. As your children grow, the rules will need to change to suit their needs. Regular family meetings will serve this purpose well. Hold them weekly, but more often if you need to.

Post the rules at kid-eye level on the refrigerator. Use writing or pictures, whichever you need for your readers and non-readers. "No parking" signs through pictures of kids yelling, etc., work well. Google has an images tab for your use in this project, or you can take pictures of the kids breaking the rules. Now you can reward both positive behaviors and the lack of rules being broken. "I notice when you were playing with Jared just now, you were not shouting. I love how you follow the rules! In fact, I think you are our champion rule-follower!" This is where your true power lies for bringing out positive behavior. When you use the power of the present moment to infuse positivity into your child's heart, it strengthens the heart-to-brain message, "I am a good kid."

At the end of the book you'll find reminder slips to post where you will see them often, so that infusing positivity soon becomes a habit. Tape them on the fridge, on the bathroom mirror, on your dashboard—anywhere your eyes frequently land. Use Heartfelt Appreciation in this form to strengthen the positive input:

"When _______ I feel _______ because _______."

Note: For preschoolers and many teens, you will use redirection more than do-overs. Redirection just means that you lead the child to the better behavior right away, rather than making an issue out of the infraction (another way of giving no attention to the infraction). For a preschooler, for example, instead of using a do-over when he is swinging his feet near the newly painted living room wall, just suggest using those feet to run around outside: "Look at those swingy feet. They have so much energy! How about taking them outside to see if they need some running time?"

For teens, please see Chapter Four in this book for hints on how to gain their cooperation. Do-overs may not be your first choice with older children.

7. **Guard your family meeting time as sacred.** If you decide on Sunday at 6:00 p.m., be sure you don't let that time commitment erode. Let the children overhear you declining other opportunities to fill the meeting time slot, just as you would decline them because of religious services or important business meetings. It will increase their sense of the importance of the meeting time, as well as the importance of their family identity. As issues come up between meetings, ask family members if they think you need an impromptu meeting. Remind the kids that they can call meetings when they see a need, as well. Your flexibility and inclusive approach also increase buy-in to the meetings and to the solutions that result from your discussion.

8. **Give the children your heartfelt appreciation for their participation in the meeting.** You can say:

   "When you participated in our family meeting, I felt like we were really a together group. It was really nice for all of us to find out what great ideas you have!"

DAY FOUR—INSTITUTING DO-OVERS FOR INFRACTIONS

Whenever a rule is broken, your *only* response is "Broke a rule. Let's have a do-over." Give no warnings, engage in no negotiations, and offer no reiteration of the rule. In other words:

- *No* saying, "One more of those and you'll be doing that over."

- *No* accepting from the child: "If I promise not to do it again, can I not have a do-over?" You: "Oh, all right, but you have to remember next time."

- *No* saying, "That was spitting and you know we have a rule against spitting."

These interactions all give attention to the infraction, which feeds the intensity-hungry brain what it wants most (your intense emotional response) and rewards the very behavior you don't want. All you want to do is stop the behavior with an intensity-free do-over. Rehearse do-overs with your child. As part of the family meeting, allow her body to feel what happens when there is an infraction.

For the rehearsal, say to your child:

> *"OK, get mad at me for taking your plate away before you were ready, and say a bad word. Then I'll say 'Broke a rule. Let's have a do-over.'" After giving you a rather puzzled but interested look, your child says the bad word. You say, "Broke a rule. Let's have a do-over." Your child repeats the scene that led up to using the bad word. Then together you run the scene over, with an appropriate response. You say, "Thank you very much for the do-over. Now let's go finish picking up those toys so we can go over to Grandma's house" (or whatever is happening next).*

Here's the "do-over formula":

1. Infraction.
2. Broke a rule. Let's have a do-over.
3. Thank you very much.
4. Redirect.

You deliver no judgment, no discussion, and no intensity. It's the same as putting out a fire by depriving it of oxygen. You want to extinguish the behavior, so you deprive it of your attention. Your child will learn several things from this, the first of which is that do-overs are not the end of the world. In fact, we can even rehearse them and play around with them a little. Second, she'll learn that you can respond to infractions without getting all riled up. And third, she'll now know exactly what will occur if she breaks a rule. That clarity helps her stay within the boundaries. And if you break a rule, by yelling or losing your temper, you can set a great example of responding to your own negative behavior by having a do-over. Yes, the kids will love that.

DAY FIVE- HEARTFELT APPRECIATION REVISITED

Continue giving your child small moments of feedback when things are going well.

"When you _______ I feel _______ because _______" creates the emotional intensity match that your child's brain desires. Remember: think of it as the equivalent of yelling, only on the positive side. It rewards the brain, so the good behavior will be repeated. Do this at least three times today.

DAY SIX—KEEPING IT POSITIVE

Wake up in the morning and ask yourself, "What can I do to bring out the good in my child today?" (This contrasts your former question, "How will I ever make it through the day with this child?") Pat yourself on the back for taking on this challenge courageously.

Giving attention to the positives you see in the present moment is so far removed from our traditional ways of changing child behavior that it requires a huge effort at the beginning. Trust that it will get easier as you practice, and that the rewards of better behavior will be so compelling that you won't have the slightest desire to return to the old ways.

Acknowledge your child's success at least four times today. If it's a rough day, think in terms of taking and encouraging baby steps; find the tiniest victory or achievement and reward it with your focused attention. Remember that, although you could choose to promote negativity by yelling today, you choose to encourage positivity by delivering your heartfelt appreciation. It will get you what you want: good behavior, peace in your relationship, and high self-esteem in your child.

DAY SEVEN—WAYS TO REMIND YOURSELF TO USE THE TECHNIQUES

If you find yourself becoming distracted from giving attention to your child for things that are going right, refer to the printed Heartfelt Appreciation reminders in the back of this book, and place them around the house, car, garage, and yard. Or if you'd prefer, just write a + (positive) sign on a sticky note, or write "remember," or draw a picture. The symbol can be something that only you know, or it can be something the kids are in on, too. It's up to you, but if the kids are in on it, they may use the notes to remind themselves to be positive with you and with each other!

Note: If you have a highly sensitive child, you may want to experiment with ways that he can accept positive feedback. I suggest writing him notes with "When you _______ I feel _______ because _______" messages on them and placing them under his pillow, or in his backpack for later discovery. If your child isn't reading yet, write the notes anyway, and read them to him at bedtime. This creates a wonderful moment of highly rewarding intimacy, centered on the good behavior you desire. You will definitely see more good behavior.

Chapter Four of this book has more on this.

DAY EIGHT—TEACHING YOUR CHILD A LESSON

Look for at least two opportunities to share your values when there is no infraction today. When you see something happen between a parent and child or siblings in the grocery store, engage your child in a quiet conversation about how "our family" does things. Remember to use what happens between the neighbors, on TV, during your work day, while driving in traffic, or what you hear in a song on the radio. Take the opportunity to share what good behavior and beliefs look like in your world, and use your family name to identify the values. "In the Jones family, we do it this way." Keep in mind that your time to teach is limited; kids grow up and move on. Use this time while they are in the "laboratory" of your home to teach them what you want them to know, and to give them the social skills you want them to have. When they leave home, you will be assured that you have given them what they need to get along in the world.

DAY NINE—HAVING YOUR CHILD EAVESDROP AS A PARENTING TOOL

Let your child overhear you discussing her successes in glowing terms with your spouse or another adult. You know how kids have radar for phone conversations? (Why is that, do you suppose? I think it's because they're learning to be adults and to have adult conversations. They need to listen very intently when you're on the phone because they only hear half of the conversation, and need to do a lot of mental processing to imagine the other half.) Use this radar to your greatest advantage to infuse further positivity into your child's heart.

Here's an example. Call your mom and say:

> *"Do you know what Gina did today? She played quietly while Evan was taking his nap, and when he woke up, she greeted him with that cute little voice she uses. He was so excited to see her! And I was thrilled to see what a caring big sister she is. Thanks for listening, Mom. I love to share the good things with you. Yes, I am really proud of her."*

Involving a third party is powerful stuff. It brings about real change by lifting up your child's sense of self in your eyes, as communicated to other people.

DAY TEN—ACKNOWLEDGING YOUR OWN SUCCESS

Begin to allow yourself to think, "I am capable of this." Notice any victories for which you can take credit. Write them down. Reward yourself by getting a sitter. Pat yourself on the back all the way to the restaurant where you're going for a celebration dinner. Don't put this one off.

DAY ELEVEN—INTERNALIZING ACCOMPLISHMENTS

Focus on how the accomplishments must feel to your child:

> *"Wow, that must feel so wonderful to have three stars on your school chart today! I bet you're feeling pretty darn good about it."*

The ultimate goal of Present Moment Parenting is to use this moment to infuse positive messages into the child, so that he eventually internalizes them.

This gets at a question I often hear: "Can you praise a child too much?" When your child's behavior has been very challenging, I believe it is more important to focus on whether your heartfelt appreciation is frequent enough, rather than whether it is too frequent. Remember that, since the challenging child has received so many negative, punishing messages that need to be counteracted, it will be quite a while before the positives will get to be too much. If you start to feel as if they are too frequent, and your child is becoming deaf to them, or they are not having the effect you wanted, back off a little, but don't stop. Use more of the internalizing suggestions in the paragraph above.

DAY TWELVE—"TESTING: ONE, TWO, THREE"

Children are scientists. They are testing to see what stays true over several trials. Develop an appreciation for this persistence, knowing that it will serve them very well as adults. (During coaching sessions, I am often conscious of the fact that I'm talking to the parents of future leaders, if we can just get them safely to adulthood!)

Because the child is a scientist who is always testing to see what stays true, your role is clear. Show him that it always stays true that he will hear heartfelt appreciation when he engages in desired behavior. And show him that it always stays true that he will be redirected or have a do-over when he breaks a rule. Simple enough. The more consistent you are with your heartfelt appreciation, redirection, and do-overs, and the more predictable the results, the sooner your child's experiment can end. The question "What will happen when I do this?" has been answered.

DAY THIRTEEN—LOVING THE CHILD YOU HAVE: GROWN-UP TASKS

Intense children are constantly getting involved in something. Sometimes it's appropriate, and sometimes it's not. The basic nature of your child, namely that she is curious and always wanting "more," will likely not change. She may be talkative, questioning, opinionated, and insistent. The positive side of these traits is that she will definitely be a "force in the world" as an adult. Today you will focus on going with your child's natural urges to get the best behavior from her. The child's greatest task is to individuate from you, which means becoming "not Mom" and "not Dad," but "me." It's an established fact that you might be successful making a person something she is not, but the chance of her growing up healthy and happy are not great if her major teacher (parent) finds her most authentic self unacceptable.

If you have an artistic child, discover ways that you need her talent (e.g., designing invitations, choosing colors for a room, arranging furniture; whatever her strength may be). And if you have a mechanical child, use her special abilities to help figure out what needs to happen if, for example, the garage door doesn't work. If you have a musical child, have her entertain you and your friends whenever possible, unless she is self-conscious about it. (Don't push her to perform if it causes her extreme discomfort. You will never foster growth in her with that tactic. Give her time and space to perform on her terms, which may be only playing for herself or family.) If you have a child that writes well, engage her talents for composing the annual family letter to friends, or have her write a letter to the editor on a topic that interests her.

Give children grown-up tasks to do whenever it is feasible. Your aim is to lift the child up to new heights: parents often tell me their children just glow when they are given grown-up tasks. The long-term effect of this tool is that children gain confidence in their own abilities, pride in their work, and an associated increase in self-efficacy. Humanity's greatest need is to be needed, not entertained, as one might derive from looking at the way we function as a society. The greatest joy is to use one's talents to make a difference in the world. I believe we have lost sight of this and it's time to turn the way we deal with children around. Think of how you want your children to evolve. Do you want them to be experienced enough to handle their own lives, or dependent on others to create their experiences for them? Please note that video games and video watching only make use of others' creativity, and only allow input. Children benefit much more from creating their own thoughts and producing their own art than being receptacles for others' creativity. A powerful formula for success is: honor the child you have and provide her with many opportunities to become more of who she is by using her natural talents.

Assign your child a title in the home. If he's good at keeping order, he's the Chief of Operations. If she's great at technology, she's the Director of Home Technology. If he does great yard work, he's the Head of Grounds Keeping. Examine which strength you want to cultivate in your child, and lift him or her up with a suitable title for the role! And if sibling says, "I'm not the director of that, so I don't have to help," be sure she knows she's the Assistant Director.

DAY FOURTEEN—HOLD THE CHILD'S SUCCESS IN YOUR HEART

A highly effective way to bring out the best in your child is to hold her successes in your heart overnight. You can say: "I was just thinking about how wonderful you were when we had company yesterday. You said 'hello' to Paul when he arrived at the door and welcomed him in. Did you know that that's one of the best things you can do with other people, show interest in them? It is a powerful skill, and you are learning it. I am so proud of you!"

Saying this the day after the incident conveys to your child that her good behavior was so impressive that you held it in your heart overnight (the way you undoubtedly used to hold bad behavior in your heart overnight.) Imagine the impact of this delayed response on your child's heart!

Your comments are forging a path in her neural pathways and feeding her self-image positive messages. They also have the effect of giving a huge dose of emotional intensity to the behavior you want! This is highly rewarding to the brain, and greatly increases the likelihood that she will repeat the positive behavior.

MY PROGRESS NOTES

Obstacles to implementing the ideas in this chapter:

Ways I will overcome the obstacles:

After using the ideas in this chapter, here's my success story:

CHAPTER THREE

Benefits of Present Moment Parenting

When you have mastered Present Moment Parenting, you are able to:

1. Understand the origin of intensity (the hungry brain)
2. Choose to see the positives in your child
3. Set firm boundaries around behavior with a cooperatively designed rule list
4. Give heartfelt appreciation for both good behaviors and the lack of breaking rules
5. Give predictable, effective consequences (do-overs)
6. Teach your values when there is no infraction
7. Honor the child you have, and assign grown-up tasks to increase self-esteem
8. Deliver heartfelt appreciation after holding accomplishments in your heart, increasing their impact

CONTINUING PAST THE FIRST TWO WEEKS: ENCOURAGEMENT FOR YOU

Give yourself time to integrate all you have read in this guide. Do not feel pressure to have it all down at the end of two weeks, but allow yourself to evolve at your own pace. And know that the power of intention can turn the drama you are experiencing at home into a scene of peace and joy. If you intend to be the child's success mentor rather than the behavior police, your effectiveness is assured. Taking that intention to the point of action, you improve the child's behavior, his sense of self, and your relationship. For more on this topic, read *The Power of Intention* by Wayne Dyer.

The excitement of having an intense child in your life does not have to change, but your emotional reactions will definitely change. You will have the thrill of enjoying a spirited kid who has joy for life and whose body has learned where the intensity matches occur: in desired behaviors. You will also feel more centered and confident as a parent. You will be able to accept credit from friends and family for the improvements, and will have many more pleasant interpersonal moments with your child. In your mind, picture the child as an adult looking back at his relationship with you. Imagine his words as he describes his growing up times with a friend:

> *"Yeah, I gave my parents a run for their money, but they were always encouraging me. They let me know when I was out of line, but in a respectful way. And they were sure to communicate what they appreciated, so I could learn to act appropriately, feel valued for who I am, and know I was really contributing. I am so grateful to them."*

You and your child are in a win-win situation!

MY PROGRESS NOTES

Obstacles to implementing the ideas in this chapter:

Ways I will overcome the obstacles:

My success story:

CHAPTER FOUR

Troubleshooting Real Life Challenges

In this chapter, you will read direct responses to specific parents' needs, as they learn to apply Present Moment Parenting. Enjoy!

DEALING WITH RESISTANCE: WHAT IF MY CHILD BALKS AT MY POSITIVE COMMENTS?

Many children have trouble receiving a positive comment because they are just not used to heartfelt appreciation coming their way. Most of the feedback they've received from adults has been corrective:

"Stop that right now."

"Go to your room (or quiet place at school)."

"I can't take your attitude one more minute."

"Can you just do one thing without arguing?"

"I'm busy right now. Don't interrupt me."

"I never said you could do that."

"Not again!"

"No! I said no, and I meant no."

"If you do that one more time, I'm going to ground you."

"I have to tell you everything a thousand times!"

These comments can be interpreted as failures in the child's heart. They all communicate that the child cannot do the right thing. If this sounds like the language your child has been hearing, it's important to note how familiar it must be to his ears and heart. If you suddenly change to saying, "I just love the way you said thank you to Julia's mom so politely today!" you will notice that your child picks up on the difference right away.

It is not necessarily always pleasant for your child to hear positive responses, as they are so different from much of the language to which he is accustomed. But it is very important to continue past this phase by expressing your appreciation of his actions. This is necessary to be successful in infusing positivity into his heart. Just say, "I know this is different from what you're used to hearing, but it's our new way of talking now, and I know you will get used to it." Communicate that "wild horses couldn't stop you" from pointing out the good things. Children eventually come to accept that this is how the new "family culture" works. Writing your positive comments in a shared notebook may further help the child accept them, as it's a little less direct. For more on sharing notebooks, see page 115 under "I See You" Letters.

WHAT IF SHE REFUSES THE DO-OVER?

An intense child frequently refuses to do the infraction over. Be ready for this by calmly deciding ahead of time that she will comply. The clearer you are about the consequence actually occurring, the more secure your child feels. And deciding that you will definitely stop the flow of intensity after an infraction will strengthen your efforts significantly. Remember to avoid warnings, reiterations of the rule, and negotiations. These all give attention to behavior you don't want. Use an unemotional, "Broke a rule. Let's have a do-over."

The do-over is not punishment. It is simply a teachable moment. Turn on the intensity as soon as the do-over has been completed. Say: "You did a great job with your do-over. I am proud of how you handled that!"

If you are consistent in the do-over expectation, your child will adjust to the new routine. Give it some time. Expect that there may be a window of time between when you say, "Let's have a do-over," and the time your child actually does it. Delivering some kind of heartfelt appreciation during the window, e.g., "You controlled your strong feelings well," often goes a long way toward lifting the child up. Communicate that you are not locked in a power struggle; you still see the good in your child and you still expect the do-over (consequence) to occur. Use predictive language to encourage the behavior you desire. Say, for example: "As soon as you're done with your do-over, will you finish helping me with these cookies?"

WHAT IF THERE'S AN ALL-OUT TANTRUM ASSOCIATED WITH DO-OVERS?

Give the tantrum no attention. Simply communicate that you have decided that the do-over is going to take place, but after the storm has passed.

With older children, privileges are frozen until the do-over is complete. No TV, phone time, video games, or computer until the do-over is done. Always use a gentle and inviting tone when setting these limits. There's no need to be harsh, and if you are, you'll trigger the child's opposition. Guaranteed.

As the child becomes accustomed to the routine, she will accept her do-overs more readily. Many children evolve to the point that they do scenes over themselves when necessary! Keep the faith, and use the do-overs routinely. Remember that confusion is very hard on an intense child, and that *being calm and communicating clearly creates security.*

DEALING WITH OPPOSITIONAL BEHAVIORS – AVOIDING TRIGGERS

Here are tips for the language to use with children who oppose you at every turn:

1. **Realize that your child has triggers that are beyond his power to overcome.** Saying "you have to" and even just "you" can serve as the triggers. Avoid the use of "you" whenever possible. Talk about what "needs to happen" instead. For example, say, "That TV needs to be off so we can enjoy our story."

2. **As a part of normal child development, your child is compelled to oppose you.** He does not know how to individuate (become fully himself) gently. He must tell you that you are wrong in order to know himself as separate from you. Your job is to teach him that he is himself, and no one else can ever be him. Appreciate his unique characteristics and make an effort to use his talents in daily living.

   For example, you might say:

   "You are so good at math. Will you help me figure out the restaurant bill?"

   "You are so good at talking to people. Will you be my phone answerer today?"

   "I love how you choose colors. Let's plan the bathroom paint job together!"

   Keep in mind that every time you speak to your child, his brain is "watching" for something to oppose. Avoid baiting his brain.

3. **Use language that forwards the action beyond the immediate event.** Mention a pleasant activity just ahead. The former keeps the focus on positives, and the latter supports his individuation by demonstrating that you trust his abilities.

   For example:

   "Brush your teeth right now, or there will be no story tonight."

   Replace with: "*As soon as you brush your teeth, I'll be ready to read your story.*"

"Get into the car right now, or we won't be getting that ice cream you wanted."

Replace with: *"When we get into the car, I'll need your help with directions to that new ice cream place."*

4. **Engage your child's problem-solving abilities rather than telling him what to do.** Ask a question instead of delivering a command.

   For example:

   "You just took the last dessert. Now you have to put that back."

   Replace with: *"Please check around and notice who didn't have dessert yet. What needs to happen next?"*

   "It's not your turn to talk right now."

   Replace with: *"What's our rule about letting other people finish speaking?"*

   This encourages your child to use his own reasoning, which leads him to be less dependent on you and trust more in his own abilities.

5. **Avoid using the child's name at the beginning of a request:** saying "Sam, you need to get your pajamas on right now!" immediately sets his brain up for opposition. His name is a trigger that you want to use sparingly when you have an expectation. Instead, say, "It's 8:00. What do you think happens now?" If he plays a "word game" with you, go ahead and entertain him with it for a while if he is the type of child

who can be "jollied" into cooperation. It's fine to use humor with your child, even when it's important that he go to bed. Levity helps people cooperate. But arbitrary treatment causes them to rebel. If he is not the type who can maintain control when you ask him, "What do you think happens now?" just say: "Time for bed, everyone! Who gets to turn off the TV tonight? Whose turn is it to turn off the lights? Who's on dog duty this week?"

This forwards the action and allows the child to cooperate without the challenge of a command.

6. **Assign a grown-up task.** See Day Thirteen.

7. **Pat yourself on the back when you are successful in following the steps above.** Give yourself small healthy rewards as you improve, e.g., take a bubble bath; let your schedule include some down time; say "no" to a possible commitment . . . and feel good about it!

   To keep up your progress with your child, you may want biweekly parent coaching appointments to help you stay on track. You'll receive encouragement and credit for the small victories as they emerge. And your coach will help you realize that your home is noticeably more peaceful. Sometimes parents are so wrapped up in problem solving that they forget to notice their own successes!

   The best part about being a parent coach is that I get to watch parents take charge of their families, even when it's hard to do. I see them getting the credit from relatives, teachers, and childcare providers for their children's improved behavior. I see them healing their relationships with their children. And I realize there's no better job in the world!

TRANSFORMING THE DIFFICULT BEDTIME

Among the parents I coach, one near-universal issue arises at some point: How do we take the pain out of bedtime? Here are some solutions to this often-frustrating everyday issue.

Set up a family meeting. Using the same approach that you would with a respected adult, ask your child if she will be available at 7:00 p.m. on Tuesday to discuss an important issue. She may even want to check to be sure she's available! That's perfectly fine. It's the same process you would go through with a respected colleague. This gives the child a sense of being respected and also infuses a feeling of importance into a troubling issue. I recommend this approach for any topic that needs discussion in your family life.

Use the meeting to lay out the issue of bedtime squabbles as objectively as you can. You might say something like, "I've noticed that we're having trouble settling down without an argument at bedtime. I know that when this happens, I get upset, and I imagine that you do, too. I would like to see us have a peaceful bedtime instead, and I am now opening up the discussion to everyone for solutions. What ideas do you have that might help our bedtime go more smoothly?"

Listen intently to everyone's input, from the oldest parent to the youngest child. Ask for clarification if something isn't clear. Write suggestions down; this helps everyone feel respected and heard. Remember, caring is defined as giving "close attention." Listening intently is a fabulous way to give everyone close attention. Don't forget to include your own suggestions as you write. Make every effort to incorporate at least one idea from each family member. There may be several good ones, and if you have too many, consider using them on alternate evenings.

Use Present Moment Parenting for creating a peaceful bedtime. Establish the bedtime rules with the child's input. Rules should start with "no": no getting out of bed once the light is out; no asking for more time; no stalling; no negotiating; no whining; no bothering your sister; no crying; no excuses. Children know what the rules are, and the ones they offer will typically be more stringent than yours. Use the child's rules religiously whenever practical, as this creates buy-in, which strengthens the likelihood that the rules will be followed. The clearer the rules, the easier it is for the child to follow them.

If a bedtime rule is broken, there is an immediate, non-negotiable do-over. A gentle, unemotional "Broke a rule. Let's have a do-over" is all that is needed. No attention (no talking, no correcting, and no negotiating) should be directed to the child's negative behavior during the do-over. If your child refuses the do-over, don't push. Let the moment pass, and say something positive about the present moment. "I know you're having a strong feeling about not going to bed right now. Thank you for telling me your feeling. I love knowing what's going on inside. I bet that you'll have some other strong feelings to tell me tomorrow, and I look forward to hearing them. Do you want to turn off the light or should I?" This shows you are attuning to your child in the present moment, which helps her feel seen, and also lets her know that bedtime is certain. Try your hardest not to use commanding or threatening language about bedtime. Think of it as pleasant for everyone, which will help your child think of it that way, too.

Requests for positive behavior should start with "I need you to" or "This needs to happen" rather than as questions such as, "Would you please . . ." or "Would you like to . . . " which imply the child has a choice. Remember, when you are clear and certain, you are giving your child a huge gift. It may take several nights of this clarity for the child to adjust to the routine, but it will be well worth the effort. Every minute you spend making this work now will pay off significantly in the future. You are teaching your child that she can go to sleep on her own just like a big person. This is very valuable information for her, as it will help her to believe in herself in other areas, too.

For steps that are completed with cooperation, use heartfelt appreciation to show that you are noticing and valuing her actions. This can be incredibly powerful and strengthens the desired behavior significantly. You might say, "I see that you have your teeth brushed and are headed for your room. Thank you so much for following our plan, Kristi. Every time you do this, I feel like you are making this house such a wonderful place to live!" Using the formula "When you _______ I feel _______ because _______" for this form of feedback makes remembering how to deliver it much easier.

Set a definite bedtime. Younger children should go to bed earlier than the older ones if there is an age difference of two years or more. Usually a half hour is ample time to separate the two bedtimes. If you have three or more children, you may want to make bedtime more uniform so that you assure your adult time at the end of the day. This is very important. Knowing that you, as a single parent or with your spouse or partner, can definitely count on some winding down time helps you to handle the challenges that will come tomorrow. Do not consider this optional. You need your time alone or time together. It is very good modeling for your children, as well. They need to know that time to oneself or as a couple is vital to healthy adult living, and that it also assures Mom and Dad will be in a good mood tomorrow.

Include whatever special rituals in the bedtime routine that the children deem important, and that are acceptable to you. Rituals might be as simple as: wash your face and brush your teeth, take a drink of water, put on pajamas, say good-night to the fish, read with Mom or Dad, and settle in for sleep. To communicate respect for your child's process, indicate that you value the ritual as much as the child does; be sure to remind her to say good-night to the fish if she forgets. Rituals are very important for children's transition to the next activity, especially at bedtime. They provide a sense of continuity and comfort, which is vitally important to raising healthy kids. Reading together is my favorite bedtime ritual, as it points out that you value reading and learning, it offers a great opportunity for snuggling, and most important, it truly allows the child to feel your slowed-down, caring energy.

Requests for extending the reading time are inevitable. It's easiest to avert this by reminding the child "only two stories" before you start, and then gently sticking with it. Make a comment such as, "It makes me so proud to see that you love to read this much, honey, but tomorrow is another day, and you can read during any free time you have. Now I need to see the light out. Good night. I love you very much." Then leave the room and consider the day with children completed (unless, of course, there is a true illness).

Note: Families who are dedicated to more peaceful bedtimes find it fun and very helpful to "rehearse" bedtime. On a Saturday afternoon, you can say, "Let's all go brush our teeth, get into our pajamas, pick out a book to read, and go to bed" and then do it. This is important because when you think about it, what has the child's bedtime experience been? Mom and Dad say, "Time for bed!" I ignore them. They say it again. I whine that I don't want to go to bed. They say it again more forcefully. I get mad at them for bossing me around and I run away . . . and on and on. They think this is bedtime, as this has been their only experience! The kids love rehearsing the new calm routine, and it creates maps in their brains that show them exactly what bedtime can look like. When the time comes to actually go to bed, the children are remembering what they rehearsed, rather than learning it for the first time. This works so much better.

Please also note that the hours of sleep needed in today's society are grossly underestimated by many people, adults and children alike. Adequate sleep helps to prevent illness, both physical and mental, and there is *no* substitute for adequate sleep if you want healthy, reasonable interactions with your family. As parents, we need to be sure our children have the sleep they need, and to also be sure our own sleep needs are met. Here are the National Institutes of Health's recommendations for hours of sleep by age:

Newborns: Sixteen to eighteen hours
Preschool-aged Children: Eleven to twelve hours
School-aged Children: At least ten hours
Teens: Nine to ten hours (note that this is not less than for younger children)
Adults (including older adults): Seven to eight hours

"Sufficient sleep is not a luxury—it is a necessity—and should be thought of as a vital sign of good health."

- Wayne H. Giles, MD, MS, director, Division of Population Health, National Center for Chronic Disease Prevention and Health Promotion

PRESENT MOMENT PARENTING WITH TEENS

Olivia's mom, Sonja, was concerned when she found out that her ninth-grader had been missing classes at school. She called me for reassurance, fearful that her daughter may be experimenting with drugs. We talked about Eckhart Tolle's "power of now" philosophy: "Nothing has ever happened in the past. Nothing will ever happen in the future. Everything happens in the present moment." I encouraged Sonja to keep this present moment in mind. What positives could she see in the girl standing before her right now? When we pay exquisite attention to the present, the future takes care of itself.

After the appointment, I wrote Sonja this follow-up list, reviewing the points we had covered in our conversation:

Because you are concerned about Olivia's lying, give heartfelt appreciation to her every time she tells the truth. Say, "When you fill me in on what's going on, I am so proud of you because it shows me we are building trust." In fact, use heartfelt appreciation whenever your teenager talks civilly to you! About anything! If you want communication, reward communication.

Support Olivia's individuation, rather than fight it. Use her talents. When writing, say, "Help me with the best way to word this." You can think of many other opportunities to do this.

Be interested in her music. Ask her questions about it, and really notice her taste. Listen through her headphones to her favorite song, and comment on the guitar riff that shows particular talent.

Deep listening without judgment is the best gift you can give a person, especially a teenager. Just say, "You're feeling really frustrated right now." Don't try to fix the problem. Just listen and reflect the feeling to Olivia.

"I trust you" is music to a teen's ears. Even if you are still in the trust-building stage, use this phrase to plant the idea that establishing trust is possible. It can be about something as small as "I trust you to choose the right words to use with your friend." Or it can be as big as "I trust you to drive the car safely." You will know what to use when.

Remember that Olivia is a scientist, testing to see what stays true over several trials.

Give her positive feedback about what a good friend she is, listening and being there when her friend needs her the most.

Keep in mind that it's a confusing time when a person has one foot in adulthood and another in childhood. The more supportive you are, the better your relationship will be.

Have regular family meetings. Use the first meeting to acknowledge everything good that you notice about each family member. Use subsequent ones to solve problems when necessary.

Attentive parents are the anti-drug and the anti-disenfranchisement agent. Even when they can't show it, teens still regard their parents as the biggest influence in their lives. Keep this in mind, and never waver from your role as your child's life guide, even when peers seem to be their only influence (this is normal child development, but it still needs parental influence to prevent it from getting out of balance). Keep the sense of belonging focused on Olivia's place in the family, in an effort to decrease her need to find inappropriate belonging with peers.

I have confidence that this will just be a phase. Sonja has done a wonderful job and Olivia is so fortunate to have her as her mom. She is a parent who really cares, and it shows.

For further information on teens and drugs, visit:
www.drugfree.org/think-child-using/your-first-step-ask/

PREVENTING KIDS FROM BEING OVERSCHEDULED

Overscheduling has been a recurrent topic in many parent coaching sessions I've recently had with clients. Here are some of the concerns expressed by parents and hints about ways to prevent getting your child too involved:

Is it OK to stay home with a twenty-month-old, where he only sees adults and doesn't have play dates?

Before the age of two or three, it's perfectly fine for adults to be the primary contacts with a child. Often very young children need developmental time before they are able to behave appropriately with other children. Although most children are exposed to peers in childcare at a much earlier age, it's perfectly fine to start introducing them to their peers when they are three. One big advantage to keeping your child close to home is he may be sick less frequently than he would be if he were exposed to other children!

Should three-year-olds take music and swimming lessons?

The age and developmental stage of the child should be the first consideration in making these decisions. A three-year-old can readily take swimming lessons, but the expectations of him in the class should be minimal. If he enjoys the water and is learning new skills without anxiety, the lessons can continue. If he's frightened, refusing to participate or do what the instructor says, feel free to wait a year or two before introducing swimming lessons again.

Is it all right to let your child quit a sport or activity?

I realize that many parents are worried that they may be raising a "quitter" if they allow their children to stop participating in a sport or musical activity. Please keep in mind that childhood is a time for exploring a variety of possibilities. Children need to be free to say yes to something, try it, and decide if they are enjoying themselves. If the activity is stressful for the child, or if she just doesn't enjoy it, it's perfectly fine to stop and look around to see what the other choices might be. The younger the child, the more fluid the decisions can be. As she grows up and commits herself to high school activities, she will likely remain more loyal to them. By then she has a better-defined sense of self, and more decision-making skills. She'll still need your guidance, so be sure to encourage her to listen to what her heart says when she's making a decision. It's more preferable to grow up learning how to honor one's true self than to continue in an activity because of others' expectations and desires.

How many nights a week should we schedule an activity?

This all depends on the age of the child, her energy level, and her school demands. If a child is very interested in sports, music, or dance, and wants to participate, it's wonderful to offer the opportunity. But be sure you limit the time spent in activities, so that her life maintains its balance. Kids need down time in order to develop their imaginations. They need to study the clouds and go looking for interesting rocks. They need to just spend time musing. If your child rarely has quiet alone time, be sure to make an effort to provide it. And this should be time without the computer, TV, or video games—just quiet alone time. If your very active child is always on the go, don't be concerned, but do create quiet family time, so that she becomes accustomed to unscheduled periods every week. If you encounter your normally active child spending time "doing nothing," appreciate it. It's a necessary thing, something to be honored and protected.

At what age can children decide on activities for themselves?

When you decide to offer a new activity to your child, give him time to get used to it, and then listen for signs of satisfaction or disenchantment. Avoid doing too much to influence his decision. Offering small encouragements to stay involved is fine, but pushing is never a good idea. Do not look at your child's sports, music, or dance as your way to gain self-esteem. Such things should always be about the child, as it's his life. If you allow him to decide what he'd like to spend his time doing, he learns a very important skill: listening to his inner voice and answering his true desires. He'll likely change interests many times throughout childhood, and the freedom to do so is vital to his healthy development. If you have spent money enrolling your child in an activity, let the money go if the child decides not to continue. It's still well spent, as your child has gained good information about himself and the activity. He has also gained decision-making skills while he still has you as a resource.

What signs of stress tell us that children are overscheduled?

Children who are tired all the time, are frequently argumentative, and act reluctant to participate in the simplest activities, are often letting their adults know that they are overscheduled. You might ask the child if life feels like "too much" but don't be surprised to hear her say no. She will feel a pull from peers or from within herself to stay involved with her activities. If you determine that the stress outweighs the benefits, exercise your parental role and make a decision to have her cut back, and also think of ways to reduce the overall stress in her life. Stress is a significant health concern in children, and they need adults to help them return to balanced lives. Do not fear letting the coach, dance instructor, or band director down. It's your job first and foremost to protect your child from being overstressed. Schoolwork and family time should take priority, and everything else needs to fall into place behind them.

WHAT YOUR CHILD CAN'T TELL YOU

You have probably heard the saying, "All behavior is communication." The more I think about this, the more I see how relevant it is to raising children. I want everyone to emblazon this where they will see it every day. Children misbehave because they lack the communication skills and insight to tell us what's really happening. It's our job to look beyond the behavior to the root feelings. In fact, I would say, "All behavior is a readable signal." This reminds us that not only is the child communicating, but that we as adults need to notice the signal and respond to it.

When a child whines, it's not because she likes the sound of whining. It's because she lacks the maturity and experience to say, "Mom, Dad, I'm frustrated right now because you're asking me to hurry for school, but I'm a kid and I'm just slower." Instead, she'll exhibit all kinds of unwanted behaviors: whining, delaying, arguing, and even getting physically aggressive.

When a grade-schooler refuses to do his homework, it's not likely that he is simply lazy. His behavior is communicating that he is discouraged in some way. Our first impulse as parents is to make him see that he needs to get the work done so he can be successful. We remind, cajole, threaten, and eventually explode. A much more helpful first impulse is to determine what to do about the discouragement.

When a teenager doesn't listen to our advice, it's not because he's just being a jerk. His behavior is communicating that he's in a new phase of development. He needs to make his own decisions, and we are inadvertently calling him incompetent whenever we advise him. He takes it as an insult every time we make a suggestion. He isn't able to say, "Mom, Dad, I appreciate that you care about me, and that you are wiser than I am. But I need to make these decisions myself because I am becoming a young adult, and that's what young adults do. Please bear with me as I struggle and even fail sometimes." Instead, he leaves the house in a huff, giving the door an extra hard slam for emphasis. We would be much better off if our first impulse was to support him in his decision-making, rather than to tell him what to do.

If you want cooperative behavior from your kids, take a shortcut by training your mind to see what's beneath the behavior. Practice seeing your child's innocence first, and working to understand what lies beneath the foul language, the time spent with the door locked, and the "interesting" style of dress. You will find a vulnerable changing child who simply doesn't have insight yet. It's our job as adults to gain this insight and act accordingly.

Rather than exhibit anger over disrespectful behavior, acknowledge there's an emotion that the child cannot express directly lying just under the surface. Kids get hurt a lot easier than most adults realize, so they are compelled to protect their tender hearts by lashing out. If we don't give them cause to protect themselves, by utilizing our clear view of what's really going on, they won't have to be so defensive.

So the next time you see a child "acting out," ask yourself what's being communicated. It will be an emotion that the child is too young or too immature to express directly, such as feelings of hurt, frustration, disappointment, hopelessness, or something else you can help to identify. Then address the child in those terms, rather than with your own irritation. Say, "You seem upset. Want to tell me what's up?" or "How about you take some time in your own room until you feel better and we can talk?" or "I remember being your age and feeling that same way. Sit down, and let's try to make this better together." You'll be getting to the root emotion rather than placing judgment on the child's behavior. Congratulations! You are on the shortcut to better communication and better behavior with your child.

WHEN YOUR CHILD LIES

Lying is a topic that really gets to many parents. It's so easy to go to the "fear place" when your four-year-old experiments with telling you something that is obviously not true.

It's a Normal Phase

First, realize that it's a developmental milestone for kids to lie. They do it because they figure out that there is such a thing as saying something that isn't true. It's that simple. They are not morally bad when they lie; they are just scientists testing their newfound information. "I am six years old," coming from a three-year-old is simply an experiment with saying "I am six years old." It comes from a new realization that everything one says may not really be so. When kids make a new discovery, they try it out. Lying is no different.

Give Minimal Attention

Your best response to your child's lie is to either joke with the child and say, "Six? I thought you were twelve!" or simply state, "You're three, remember?" The other alternative is to just smile and let it go. This is not deceitful lying. The thing you don't want to do is give any emotional intensity to the lies, which would assure you that the lying continues.

When children get older, you can tell when the intent is to truly deceive in order to avoid responsibility. All children do it, so please don't think your child is unique. Again, your best response is to not overreact. Keep the experimenting scientist in mind, and simply say, "We know you didn't brush your teeth. I'll meet you in the bedroom for a story as soon as you have them all shiny." This last part is called "forwarding the action." It helps kids realize you are not buying their story, and that you are not giving the lie any attention by staying stuck on it. You are moving on to the next thought, and the next activity, and you expect that they will follow.

Social Lying

As she moves into the middle-school years, you might find your child in a dilemma about when to tell a small lie in order to avoid hurting a friend's feelings. She will get invited to her best friend's house immediately after accepting an invitation to the home of a lesser-known peer. Let her struggle with this one; don't jump in to resolve it right away. And don't think there is only one right answer. The desire to be with her best buddy overrides everything else at this age, so she'll likely choose her best friend. You might see it go either way, but again, try not to get too involved in the outcome. Natural consequences are great teachers in these situations, and kids' relationships are quite fluid.

Your child may snub another child, but three weeks later be her close friend. Allowing them to work it out while you are there to listen and offer support is really the best strategy. Give your child heartfelt appreciation whenever she communicates openly with you and makes a good decision. It's all part of the growing-up process. You might want to talk about empathy, but do it at another time. When the situation is ripe, the emotions are usually too high to make a point about social graces. A car ride is the perfect setting, when things are calm, to bring this up, saying, "I was just thinking about how you and Maya are getting along better now.

How was that for you when things weren't smooth, and what did you do to make it better?" Inquiry invites the child's own wisdom to surface, and it's wonderful to behold. When there's no lecture or judgment, it encourages the child to come to you with her issues.

Tap Your Child's Experience

Ask your child what he learned about his last experience with lying. Maybe someone else lied to him, and he wants to say how that felt. This is perfect soil for planting empathy. And don't expect him to be perfect with it right away. Learning empathy is a process, not a one-time lesson.

Grow Truth-Telling

Be sure to give your heartfelt appreciation every time your child tells the truth! For example, say, "When you tell me the truth about throwing rocks outside, I really appreciate it, because it shows me how honest you are! Now let's do that over, and then we'll go put those rocks back where they belong." Use the phrase, "In our family, we say what's true," or "The Grahams tell the truth, don't we?"

Children who have experienced trauma frequently lie as a survival technique. Their past experience tells them that telling the truth is dangerous, so they fabricate to avoid being threatened. Be patient with this, and just gently say, "We know you were at the bus stop a little late today. No problem. Let's figure out how to get you to school now." If you give a lot of your emotional energy to lying, you will see it again. Make an effort to underplay lying and overplay truth-telling, in order to grow the truth-telling.

Be the Young Scientist's Laboratory Findings

Again, as a rule of thumb, underreacting to lying while stating what you know is true (or is likely true) will be your approach to lying. Just keep the scientists in mind, and give them the findings you want them to discover. Your response to lying should be an unemotional correction with no intensity. And keep in mind that kids are learning everything from you, so if you want them to learn honesty, exhibit honesty!

LOOK FOR SENSORY INTEGRATION ISSUES

Parents frequently feel mystified by their children's extreme behavior, not realizing that sensory issues are at play. These hidden factors are very often the reason for tantrums, attempts to control others, the use of harsh language, and meltdowns. Kids with sensory integration disorder have difficulty integrating what their senses tell them, so they can't move on to the next activity. A child with auditory sensory issues, for example, is unable to readily integrate sounds, which makes even ordinary sounds upsetting to her. This can cause her to be highly distracted in a classroom setting, but better at home, where the noise level is lower. Such a child might get off the bus and collapse into tears of pain and frustration, leaving her parents confused and irritated. The noise in the classroom, in the cafeteria, on the playground, and on the bus has overwhelmed her, so she becomes totally out of control by the time she arrives home.

Children who cover their ears when a train goes by or in response to other loud noises, and who then exhibit anger, rage, and disrespectful behavior, may be suffering from auditory sensory disorder. They hear the sounds of everyday life much more acutely than does the average person, and they are essentially tortured by those sounds. "Normal" sounds can be equivalent to the booming of bombs going off all around them. No wonder they melt down.

Some children have visual sensory integration disorder. They are extremely sensitive to light, and often come totally unglued in a room with fluorescent lighting. These children can see the lights vibrating at a speed that is undetectable to most people. This results in utterly understandable misbehavior in the classroom.

Other children have tactile sensitivity. They insist on soft fabrics, and can't stand the tags in their clothes or the seams in their socks. They are often extremely picky about the length of their pants or sleeves. If the tactile sensitivity affects the mouth, the children can't stand the texture of certain foods. They will be very picky eaters, again often mystifying their parents.

It's never a good idea to try to talk your child out of being particular about sensory sensitivity, or to punish him for tantrums related to sensory input. Occupational therapists in private practice can help your child with sensory issues, teaching his body to more readily integrate what his senses tell him. Ask your family doctor or pediatrician for an OT recommendation. And try to accommodate your child's needs as they arise. He truly can't make himself accept loud noises, tags in clothes, highly textured foods, or fluorescent lights by force of will. He needs professional intervention to overcome these obstacles to living a happy life, and just as important, he needs your understanding. You won't be spoiling your child by buying soft clothes, helping him protect his ears, or letting the broccoli go. In these cases, accommodations are simply compassionate.

Food sensitivities can also have a significant impact on children's behavior. Sensitivities are often not full-blown allergies, so their identification may be missed by typical allergy testing. However, the effects of food sensitivities on behavior can be severe, so it may serve you well to explore them. If you've "tried everything" and your child still melts down or becomes aggressive at the slightest provocation, consider a food evaluation by your pediatrician or naturopath. Some chiropractors and homeopaths are also well versed in food sensitivities, so the choices are broad. Doing some online research can lead you to the type of care with which you feel most comfortable. For a pediatrician's view of this issue, reference *Is This Your Child?* by Dr. Doris Rapp.

A LOVING MOM'S VICTORY

Belinda is the devoted mother of a home-schooled, brilliant seven-year-old. Her son, Andrew, is inquisitive, determined, and always ahead of the game. In fact, Andrew is a very powerful child who has so many leadership qualities that he struggles to understand why he is not in charge of both his family's life and all his interactions with his peers. When, for example, he's disagreed with his mom's restaurant choice, this little boy, one who is quite sensitive to ambient noise, has said, "If I go where you want to go it will hurt my ears. Is that what you want?" On other occasions, he's said, "If we go with Grandma and Grandpa, there will be four happy people and one unhappy person (me)."

Andrew's impulsive behavior and attempts at controlling his environment, like making his parents and grandparents cave in to his desires, has often proved overwhelming for everyone; Belinda has found herself in an increasingly exhausting battle. When things haven't gone well, Belinda has employed her default nagging, yelling, pleading, explaining, and punishing techniques, all to little avail. Belinda recognized that she needed help dealing with her challenging child.

After two coaching sessions, Belinda began to see that it's much better for Andrew if she holds the line on her decisions. Instead of pleading, explaining, and teaching, she's learned to remain very calm and to give him a choice, such as: "You can go with us and act politely, or you can eat dinner here alone in your room before we go out." On one particular occasion, Andrew quickly chose the restaurant option. As it turned out, they were seated in the noisiest spot of the dining room, and Andrew never complained a bit. In contrast to what was stated above about not asking children to simply "overcome" their sensory issues, Belinda ran an experiment: Is the sensory issue this strong, or are we at the point of Andrew just enjoying the control? She tested him and found out that he could tolerate the restaurant. In fact, Belinda realized by reading his body language that Andrew was relieved when she didn't allow him to take the reins regarding the restaurant decision. This is a perfect example of how "staying in the parent place" results in better behavior and smoother interactions. Powerful kids are relieved when their parents don't give in. Deep inside, they know their parents need to make decisions, and when that happens smoothly and without struggle, they feel secure and can let go of trying to control the situation. Belinda's sticking with her plan and offering Andrew a choice opened the door for Andrew's cooperation.

In another incident, Belinda took Andrew shopping for a birthday present for his twin friends who were turning nine. When Andrew was confronted with the fact that the shopping trip was not going to involve buying anything for him, he melted down. "You don't care about me! Why should we pay attention to just them?" he shouted. Belinda was able to realize that paying attention to Andrew's protest was not going to get better behavior from him, so she got creative. As Andrew was having his tantrum in the very crowded checkout line, Belinda excused herself from the line for a minute, reminding Andrew to have a do-over while simultaneously holding their place. Staying close enough to assure Andrew's safety, Belinda wisely removed herself from the fray, even as she gave Andrew the "grown-up task" of holding their place in line.

When they got to the car, Andrew launched a similar tantrum. Belinda calmly explained that he could go to the birthday party if he was willing to take his good attitude with him, or he could miss the party and go home. She didn't argue, nag, or ask him why he couldn't improve his attitude; she just offered him a straightforward choice. Good attitude = go to the party. Not-so-good attitude = go home. Belinda was prepared to take Andrew home, being wise enough to only offer choices she was willing to carry out.

Andrew opted to take his good attitude to the party. And when he got there, he held himself together in a way that caused Belinda to stare in amazement. As the children were gathered in a raucous group, she stood ten feet away and watched in awe as Andrew stood up in the crowd, opened his mouth to say something he shouldn't, thought a minute, closed his mouth, and sat down.

A few moments later, a high-energy girl with whom Andrew was very familiar approached him, announcing, "Your present stinks!" Andrew refused the bait, further amazing his mom.

When reflecting on Belinda and Andrew's story, it's just as important to examine what caused Andrew's good behavior as it is to look at what causes his negative behavior.

Here are some things to think about:

With Belinda's new parenting, Andrew's body reacts in a new, healthier way.

As Belinda remembers to avoid matching negative intensity by nagging Andrew, she opens the door to Andrew's relaxation around conflict. She simply offers him a choice, or says, "Broke a rule. Let's have a do-over." For Andrew, there's no more of the adrenaline rush that formerly fueled arguments. Andrew's neurological system, once accustomed to the physiological over-response that resulted from confrontation, now enjoys peace. His ability to comply with Belinda's requests is greatly enhanced when the extreme peaks of tantrum-inducing emotion are not part of his everyday routine. Further, he feels more secure because of the predictability of his mom's calm response and his planned-ahead do-over. In fact, his new physiological response is directly related to the do-over behavior that they have *rehearsed in advance*. The rules and do-overs were established during a family meeting, so there is no surprise in the interaction. Instead of experiencing an adrenaline rush, Andrew's body knows to respond calmly when his mother remains calm and reminds him of their do-over plan. He is even showing signs of reminding himself, as evidenced by his extreme self-control at the birthday party!

Belinda has gained confidence.

The more Belinda witnesses Andrew's transformation, the more deeply entrenched her new responses become. She sees Andrew's ability to control his strong urges rising from the ashes of their formerly tempestuous relationship, and she knows that she is causing the improvements.

For example, Belinda realized that Andrew was greatly relieved when she took the reins during the restaurant decision. She knew she was helping to create this very positive emotional response in her child, which helped her remember to repeat that "rein-taking" behavior. Belinda's rein-taking was directly linked to Andrew's increasingly positive behavior. When he realized that his mother was holding the reins, he was freed up to exert his own self-control. He even built on his sense of self-control when standing to speak at the party and thinking better of it, and by refusing to get involved when a child confronted him with a direct insult about his gift. Andrew's response instilled a degree of pride that Belinda hadn't felt for a long time.

Belinda trusting Andrew to do his behavior over in line at the store, while serving a grown-up purpose (holding their place in the line), enhanced his sense of his own usefulness. Note that he went from being furious about not getting a present to being helpful in a new way, all in a span of a few moments. Experiencing appropriate power is vital for intelligent children. Giving Andrew a grown-up task was the best thing Belinda could have done to lift him to a higher level of confidence in his own abilities. Further, Belinda's trust in Andrew enhanced her own confidence in her parenting skills. She walked away feeling victorious.

Please note the phrases used in the discussion of Belinda's experience:

> *"She knows that she causes the improvements."*
>
> *"She knew she was helping to create this very positive emotional response in her child."*
>
> *"Andrew's response amazed Belinda and instilled a degree of pride she hadn't felt for a long time."*
>
> *"Belinda's trust in Andrew enhanced her own confidence in her parenting skills."*

Another way to communicate trust to your child is to say, "I trust you to . . . " (treat your sister with respect; get your room cleaned up for company; make a good decision about what to wear to the party; finish your work so that you have the weekend free.) Children with high abilities may not be aware of their abilities, and may be feeling unsure of themselves. If you place your trust in the highly capable child, she learns to trust herself, which is what she ultimately needs for a healthy adult life. As her parents, you are in a unique position to do this, tapping your child's strengths in a way that others are not equipped to do.

Keep in mind that very bright children are often vulnerable. When they are not recognized for their high intellectual abilities, they often act out, as they are not feeling seen (and their survival feels at risk at a fundamental, often unconscious level). As they act out, they are accused of being highly manipulative, which only furthers their sense of isolation. A vicious cycle can develop, and the gifted child is suddenly depressed, angry, and seeking revenge. Parents can stop this cycle by truly seeing their highly capable children for who they are. This takes some doing, as many parents find themselves in uncharted waters with their gifted children.

Gifted children have "enormous capacity for novelty." They tend to apprehend and move on, apprehend and move on . . . to the point that they are sometimes misdiagnosed with attention deficit hyperactivity disorder (ADHD.) Fulfilling their intellectual needs, providing novelty and complexity on a daily basis, can be daunting and sometimes exhausting, but it is vital for the child's emotional well-being. Seek support from a gifted parents' group, organized in the community or through your school district. Parent coaching, a.k.a. individualized parent education, can also help you navigate this challenging situation.

If you are the parent of a bright, intense child, you know how hard it is to stay ahead of him or her. Hopefully, Belinda's story has inspired you, and has given you the knowledge that you don't need to be stuck in a power struggle with your child, alternately playing the heavy and giving in. You deserve to have control of your family life—and you can have it! With this approach, Belinda is well on her way to success, relief, and confidence.

MY PROGRESS NOTES

Obstacles to implementing the ideas in this chapter:

Ways I will overcome the obstacles:

My success story:

CHAPTER FIVE

Using Restorative Justice with Present Moment Parenting

When the do-over doesn't seem like "enough of a consequence" for the more serious infraction, you can teach your children restorative justice, which puts the emphasis on repairing the harm caused by the offender. Restorative justice includes all those involved in the incident, which is healing for the offender and the victim. The offender doesn't have to live with the mark of the offense in his heart. The victim has her sense of fairness restored when the offender takes steps to make amends.

These techniques can be used to resolve issues between siblings, peers, and children and adults. As parents, you'll "work yourselves out of a job" by teaching children to resolve conflict on their own. No more spending your time refereeing squabbles and trying to reason with upset kids. The offender will have a do-over immediately after the infraction, and when the feelings have settled down a bit, you'll use the present moment to employ restorative justice.

And just as with the do-over in the face of an infraction, you will set the example by using restorative justice yourself.

FAMILY MEETING STEPS

First, use a family meeting to discuss restorative justice, teach it to the children, and rehearse it. Only employ this technique after teaching it directly:

1. The offender and the offended sit face-to-face. The offender tells what it felt like to offend. ("I was really mad and it felt good to hit you because you took my stuff and wouldn't give it back.")

2. The offended tells what it felt like to be hurt.

   ("It really, really hurt when you hit me. My arm is still sore and swollen. My feelings are hurt, too, because you shouldn't do that!")

3. Together they decide how to make up for the offense. The conversation might go like this:

   Cara: I think you should do my after-dinner chores for a week.

   Owen: A week? That's too long for a little hit on the arm. How about four days?

   Cara: How about five? And I'll help a little on the fifth day.

   Owen: OK.

With this exercise, you have taught the children that:

- They, and not you, are in charge of resolving their conflicts. You will give no emotional intensity for negativity.
- Justice can be restored, and the infraction doesn't have to stay with either of them.
- They have a known, predictable method for resolving issues and are expected to use it.

Just as with do-overs, no privileges will be allowed until the mutually agreed-upon solution has been decided.

In the case of stealing from a store or damaging someone's property, the same procedure applies. The child sits with the adult owner, says what it felt like to offend, and listens as the owner expresses his feelings on the incident. Together they decide what will occur to make amends. The child may have a hard time accepting the agreement. If it's reasonable, support him or her in accepting it.

With rehearsal in advance, you have greatly increased the chance of compliance. By employing restorative justice in the face of significant conflict yourself, you will also support your children in their success. You now have an established system for dealing with conflict in your family. It's up to you to enforce restorative justice whenever a disagreement results in severe emotional or physical injury. With the use of this calm, low-intensity approach, you'll have yet another great reason to feel proud of your family as they resolve issues by coming together as skilled problem solvers!

MY PROGRESS NOTES

Obstacles to implementing the ideas in this chapter:

Ways I will overcome the obstacles:

My success story:

CHAPTER SIX

Trauma-Effective Parenting

Parenting is often complicated by events that are outside of our control. If you're parenting a child who was adopted (even at birth), who is or has been in foster care, or who has experienced abuse or neglect, it may be more challenging due to the often-subconscious impact of these events on behaviors and relationships. The same is true if you or your partner have experienced these traumas.

When parenting a child who has had early childhood trauma or adverse childhood experiences (more on these later in the chapter), normal daily interactions can trigger fear responses or "trauma responses." Trauma responses occur when the stimulus is much smaller than the response. For example, you may say, "We're all going to the park now. Can you get your bike out of the garage?" And your child may respond as though you said, "We're never going to the park again, and I'm throwing your bike away!" Reactions can come out of nowhere and seem extreme, given the preceding seemingly innocent statement. Although there may be several reasons for this kind of response, one common reason is that the event in the present moment has triggered memories of the past when your child felt unsafe.

In fact, this is how trauma works. A past event makes a person feel like he might die or be hurt—and for a child, this is any time he is not safely connected to a permanent, loving caregiver. Something in the present moment (a smell, sound, taste, motion, emotion, sight) triggers that time from the past when he felt as though his life was as risk, which brings all of the fear/rage/shame from that event into the present moment. This is why the reaction seems disproportionate, because it is not in response to the current stimulus, but to one from an earlier time.

Children must have the protection of a caregiver, or their lives are at risk. When they don't have this connection, their brains tell them that they are "in it on their own," but they know that they don't have the means to ensure their own survival. They go into "survival brain," become hyper-vigilant, and see everything and everyone as a threat. They act as though someone is trying to kill them and they have inadequate defenses.

This reaction occurs when children do not feel safe, lovable, and able to trust someone to meet their needs. It is important to feel lovable because if a child is not lovable, then the caregiver cannot be counted on to reliably do the hard work of raising the child, sometimes sacrificing their own survival needs to meet those of the child, e.g., giving up sleep to stay awake all night with a newborn. The impact of this experience is life-long, and adults who didn't have their needs met as children can be anxious, sad, reactive, explosive, and prone to trauma responses. Sometimes parenting can trigger an adult's earlier trauma, especially when the child is the same age as the parent was when his or her trauma occurred, or if the child exhibits behaviors similar to those of the person who caused the trauma.

Understanding how "having one's needs met" affects functioning is vital to helping children build their resources. When their basic needs are unfulfilled, children cannot generally respond to help. Establishing a secure home, emotional safety, and a known routine can begin the healing process. Beyond this, specific techniques for healing trauma are necessary to bring about lasting peace for the child.

MASLOW'S HIERARCHY OF NEEDS

Abraham Maslow created the following chart to explain the hierarchy of needs that affects all people. The more support you have, the more your potential can be realized. In addition, if basic needs—those on the lower part of the triangle—are not met, then higher order tasks such as relationships, creativity, meaning, purpose, and hope cannot be achieved.

And if you don't have your basic needs met (air to breathe, food to eat), nothing else matters. If you have those needs met but you aren't safe, again, nothing else matters. So after ensuring we meet those basic survival needs, everything we do with children who have experienced trauma must lead to physical and psychological safety. If children are in pain, hungry, exhausted, or feeling unsafe, all bets are off in controlling their behavior.

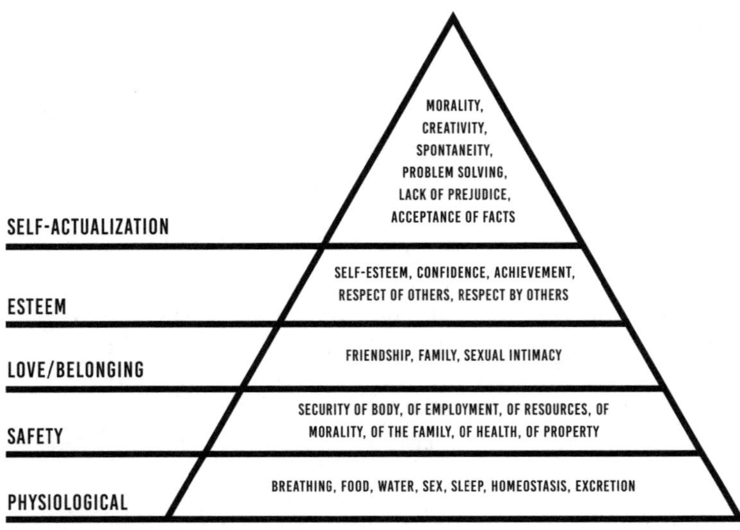

MASLOW'S HIERARCHY OF NEEDS

When a child has experienced the drug abuse or death of a parent; divorce or separation; prolonged illness and medical procedures; neglect; or the uprooting of home life due to war, sexual abuse, emotional abuse, or physical abuse, her level of need fulfillment should be one of the first things considered. If she has not had her physiological needs met, it is not realistic to expect her to behave well. Her limbic system and amygdala are signaling a survival threat, so all her energy goes into staying alive. If her safety needs are not met, the same applies. She cannot be expected to respond to discipline or relationship building when she's not feeling emotionally or physically safe. Only when love and belonging are established will the child be able to connect and grow. The issue is not the child's behavior, which is the common focus. The issue is the child's message, being communicated by the behavior, and how adults can respond in order to make negative behavior unnecessary by fulfilling the need to be held in safety.

Note: The same is true for parents. As adults, we also need to be physiologically, emotionally, and financially safe to be effective in our roles. When the factors in the lower two tiers of the pyramid are not fulfilled, parents struggle to benefit from coaching, even when they have the desire to do better for their children. Coaches are alert to parents' needs and will recommend mental health therapy, social services, yoga, journaling, therapeutic massage, self-regulation techniques, and other resources, all as complements to coaching.

It is also critical for parents who have had their own traumatic experiences to seek support in healing them. Otherwise, there's a risk of inadvertently passing on the effects of their trauma to their children through something called "carried trauma." Carried trauma exists when adults who have not healed their own trauma carry it on to their children. The resulting wounds are expressed through the parent's inability to manage emotions, having bursts of anger, rage, or shame. Trauma has been shown to be "contagious," meaning it is passed on unconsciously by spending time with someone who has trauma, i.e., living with someone who is anxious or depressed can create anxiety or depression in you. You may be experiencing this if you are sad and you don't know why, or if you're angry and you don't understand the cause—even if you otherwise have a pretty great life.

Self-regulation is the neurological and psychological ability to maintain and regain balance in the face of fear, strong emotions, stimulation, change, and new learning. One of the best things we can do for our kids is our own healing work, enhancing our ability to self-regulate and remain calm in the face of our child's tantrum or misbehavior. For toddlers, whose emotions drive their actions, and for children of all ages with trauma, we serve as "co-regulating partners." This means that in the absence of their calm, we mirror calm and share our own regulation as a set point for them to regain control. Our own self-care, rest, and healing work are critical to being able to provide the safety and healing that children from hard places need in order to thrive. Their trauma occurred in the context of a relationship, likely with someone who was supposed to protect them, so their healing must come from a safe, reliable, nurturing place. Our parenting needs to promote safety—physical *and* psychological. For children, safety comes in the form of a safe, loving, permanent relationship with a caregiver.

GRIEF, LOSS, AND TRAUMA

> *"Feeling unlovable is trauma. As children, we are dependent on our caregivers for our basic needs and survival. When we are unlovable, our very survival is put at risk."*
>
> –Brené Brown, PhD

> *"Children experience trauma which results in losses that must be grieved."*
>
> –Darla Henry, PhD

> *"The number one most stressful event for a child is the death of a parent. Number two is to be separated from a parent."*
>
> –Norma Ginther, MSW, LISW

These quotes come from people who have done years of research in the field of trauma-informed care for children, and have worked toward improved outcomes for those children. Darla Henry covers some of the principles reflected in this book with her 3-5-7 Model, revealing that unless grief, loss, and trauma are effectively processed, behavior cannot improve, peace of mind cannot be achieved, and relationships cannot be functional. In fact, we know that healthy brains turn off their ability to connect after multiple, unresolved losses. This is simply a protective mechanism. If a child looks up to his parents, upon whom he is dependent for survival, and they are not able to fulfill their parenting role, the brain takes over and says, "You're on your own, kid." If physical, emotional, or sexual abuse have accompanied this neglect, the effect is compounded exponentially. From there, the child has an internal mechanism that keeps him from depending on an adult again—the brain has learned to avoid connecting with adults because of the deep pain generated by their inability to fulfill the child's needs, or because of the profound fear they cause. This is commonly referred to as reactive attachment disorder, but it is in fact, a survival adaptation, not a disorder.

Again, this applies to adults and children alike. Our society frowns on "getting help" with grief, loss, and trauma, upholding a false image of strength in those who simply soldier on through the pain. But invariably, the pain will make itself known, coming out in drug abuse, alcoholism, gambling, screen addiction, obsessive-compulsive behavior, perfectionism, aggression, high anxiety, or any other variety of unhealthy behaviors. If as you read this, you recognize that you are an adult whose trauma and resultant behavior are affecting your child's life, do not hesitate to seek help. Your child depends on you to bring your best self to your role as a parent, in order that he may live a healthy life, have nurturing relationships, and avoid some of the effects of trauma himself.

Losses, both big and small, are normal experiences that happen to everyone on a regular basis. We give meaning to losses as we experience them, and that meaning is actually the source of our suffering. But their effect does not have to be permanent.

THE ACE STUDY AND RESULTS OF TRAUMA

Early childhood trauma has been measured through a study called the Adverse Childhood Experiences Study (ACE Study) which was conducted in 1995-1997 by the Centers for Disease Control and Prevention (CDC). The ACE Study included more than 17,000 middle-class Americans in San Diego who were college-educated, white, employed, and had good health insurance; a very privileged group. Adverse childhood experiences (ACEs) were described as: moments of physical, sexual, and verbal abuse; physical and emotional neglect; having a family member who is depressed or diagnosed with other mental illness; having a family member addicted to alcohol or another substance; having a family member in prison; witnessing a mother being abused; and losing a parent to separation, divorce, or another reason.

Two-thirds of the 17,000 people in the ACE Study had a score of at least one adverse childhood experience, and 87 percent of those who had at least one ACE had two or more. When participants reached four or more ACEs, the negative outcomes reflected significantly more concern. Eighteen US states have done their own ACE surveys; their results are similar to the CDC's. You can take the ACE Survey at www.acestoohigh.com.

The ACE Study showed a stunning link between childhood trauma and the chronic diseases people develop as adults, as well as social and emotional problems, including: heart disease, lung disease, alcoholism and alcohol abuse, illicit drug use, early initiation of smoking, adolescent pregnancy, sexually transmitted diseases, being the victim of intimate partner violence, suicide attempts, and much more. As the number of ACEs increases, so does the risk of health, social, and emotional problems.

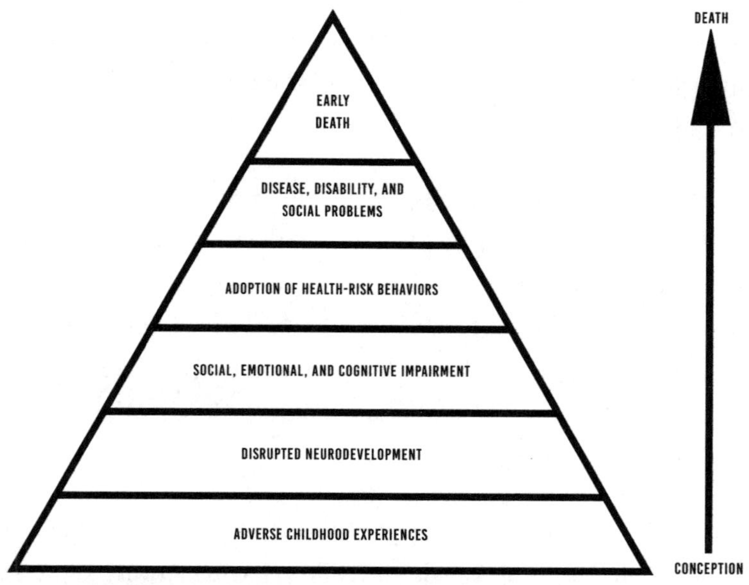

MECHANISM BY WHICH ADVERSE CHILDHOOD EXPERIENCES INFLUENCE HEALTH AND WELL-BEING THROUGHOUT THE LIFESPAN

THE TRAUMATIZED BRAIN

The brain of a child who has been traumatized by abuse or neglect undergoes changes that are detectable on scans. The child looks up to the caretakers who do not do their job of keeping him or her safe, and the brain changes dramatically. If this happens repeatedly through neglect, suddenly through trauma, or both, the brain changes take hold. The brain's amygdala (the survival alarm) goes on overdrive. It says, "The caretakers didn't do their job, so you're on your own to survive," which makes sense, as survival is the most compelling human drive. This manifests in behaviors of children who have the diagnosis reactive attachment disorder, which is really reactive attachment adaptation, as it is truly an adaptive mechanism that assures survival. The amygdala over-fires in a true attempt to help the child survive, and it doesn't have a modulating mechanism on its own. You won't see improvements unless the child is helped by someone who knows specifically what to do.

These children say to adults, "You don't love me, you've never loved me!" as the amygdala has caused them to reject that "hot stove" of what people have labeled "love." They're not going to touch it again. Their behavior reflects that they feel threatened by the attention given to other children in their midst. The amygdala is saying, "If that other child gets attention, you aren't being seen and you won't survive."

This is not a choice on the part of the child, so saying, "Make a better choice" is misdirected. The child is having a stress response similar to a reflex when a hammer is applied to the knee in the doctor's office. She cannot make a decision for the amygdala to not do its job. The front of the brain is where the decision-making part exists, and that part is not activated when the child feels threatened. For many children, their front brain is delayed in developing, often by many years, so if teachers feel a traumatized child is not acting her age, that's right. Trauma causes developmental brain delays. Some experts are calling this "brain damage" and I think this is accurate. See Dr. Bessel van der Kolk's *The Body Keeps the Score.* Also refer to Dr. Bruce Perry's work at childtrauma.org.

I also liken the stress response to a seizure. Again, the child has no control over whether the amygdala is going to fire, just as she doesn't have control over seizures. Often this happens in a seemingly innocuous situation, where the adults scratch their heads to figure out how the response was triggered. The child was just asked to put the balls in the bin, and suddenly she's screaming, "You can't make me. You don't care about me! You're a _______!" and flailing on the floor as if someone attacked her. The amygdala is trying to help the child survive, but it can't discern real danger from simple requests, and it over-fires the alarm system, telling the child she's not safe. Therefore, the reaction is out of proportion to what's occurring.

So the way to help the amygdala calm down is to remain calm when the storm occurs, and scrupulously avoid using consequences for something over which the child had no control. To "consequence" the child only further proves to her brain that you don't care, as it is always perceived as unjust punishment. And you will notice that consequences never work. They don't engage the decision-making front brain in the way one might expect, but further inflame the amygdala. Stress hormones such as adrenaline and cortisol are also released into the child's bloodstream, making the alarm response very difficult, if not impossible to overcome.

When the storm has subsided, the child needs comfort, not judgment and punishment.

Also, it's very helpful to guide the child in her grief and loss work when things are calmer. This involves assisting her to express her feelings of grief and abandonment directly instead of indirectly. Say, "If I guess how you were feeling when I asked you to put away the balls, will you tell me if I'm right or wrong?" "OK."

"I think you felt as if I was trying to control you and you really didn't want someone to control you." "Right." "Thank you for telling me." This deep "seeing" of the child assures the amygdala of survival. "When the caretakers *see me,* I'm going to survive. When they don't, my survival is threatened." So the antidote to the stress response is *seeing* the enormous emotions of the child whose amygdala is over-firing. When the amygdala is calmed down, the front brain can be activated, but the two will not operate at the same time. In other words, a traumatized child will not be making better decisions while the amygdala is sounding the alarm, often seemingly "irrationally." What we need to understand is the overreaction makes perfect sense to the amygdala, which has not developed a modulating mechanism—its function is to assure survival and it only has one setting: *on.*

REGULATING THE TRAUMATIZED BRAIN

According to Dr. Anne Gearity, children must have co-regulating partners to learn how to regulate—parents who rock or say "sh-h-h-h" or sing to little ones to help them find calm. But most traumatized kids haven't had this kind of co-regulating partner. Our kids get stuck in the "on" position. The trauma is over, but the response remains. Relationships help to regulate, and according to Gearity, for kids who have experienced trauma, behaviors are used to regulate or shift the pain into interpersonal relationships. We get so caught up in trying to change behaviors, that we miss their stories; we lose their perspectives.

Here, we'll cover some known traumatic experiences for children, keeping in mind that everything is a matter of degrees. Some mild versions of these events can cause trauma in vulnerable children, and some more resilient children can come away with no effects.

First, the value placed on the child by parents or caregivers is a major factor. If the child is only valued for her academic performance or her sports acumen, she will have a skewed view when she grows into forming her self-image. A powerful way to avoid harm in this area is to stay away from comparing her to others, and to help her see her personal progress over time.

Second, if the child is overly protected or not protected enough, he can be left without internal resources to navigate his life, or without a sense of fundamental safety. Far from being intuitive, this is something parents need help in learning over time. Each child is different in his ability to take on new challenges, and it's often hard to gauge the appropriate level of self-sufficiency. Watching your child carefully and seeing what he's feeling the urge to do can be one guideline. But when he wants to take on more than he should, it's good to consult someone who can help with the decisions. Keep in mind that *every* parent struggles with this issue, and we all follow our children's leads as they grow. Your pediatrician, nurse practitioner, or parent coach can help with these changing stages of childhood. For an online resource on child development, see www.childdevelopmentinfo.com, a CDC website.

Third, the issue of perfectionism sometimes comes into play. We tend to want our children to look good in the world, as it feels that their behavior reflects on us as parents. And we all grew up in families with "good" and "bad" kids, or we saw them in our neighborhoods. No "bad" or "good" label fits any one child, as they all go through stages of being upset and feeling settled. Traumatized children are much more likely than those without trauma to look like bad kids. They act out, get angry when corrected, use bad language, wall themselves off from others, and display profound disrespect. For parents looking at their own reputations, the judgment that can come from these children's behaviors feels overwhelming. On top of the effects of trauma, the child also develops anxiety over how people will react, which only results in controlling behaviors, making the situation worse. With all children, whenever you see unwanted behavior, think of it as an expression of pain ("pain-based behavior") rather than "bad" or "disrespectful." If you get to the true feelings of your child, teaching him that his feelings matter, he's seen by you, and he's safe with you, you will make the negativity dissipate. Then you won't need to be concerned about how he looks in the world, as he's functioning the way a safe person does, with respect and calm.

Fourth, when a child seems too dependent, you may ask, "What fundamental need could I fulfill that will relieve this dependence and help him toward self-efficacy?" Children are overly dependent because they haven't learned how to depend on themselves. A major task of parenting is building self-efficacy, so that children understand their own role in fulfilling their needs. Children who have been abused or neglected often stay dependent longer, for lack of an insightful adult who understands this need, and because trauma hinders normal development.

Fifth, helping the child return to a calm state and controlling strong impulses is vital to setting the stage for an emotionally healthy life. When a child lacks impulse control, adults become alarmed and seek ways to "make him stop." A lack of impulse control can lead to inappropriate and dangerous behavior, so it's understandable that adults may be concerned. Children who have experienced abuse, neglect, and big losses are often plagued by a lack of control over their urges. Coaches can teach compassionate direct teaching methods for controlling impulses so parents can, in turn, teach them to children.

1. Deep breathing—parents can hold or be near the child to co-regulate. This means taking deep breaths together.

2. Yoga—classroom teachers whose students are learning yoga and meditation at school are seeing sharp declines in the need to discipline.

3. Watching and breathing with the movement of an expandable ball (Hoberman sphere) can bring a child to a calm state.

4. Watching the glitter in a toy wand until it completely settles to the bottom can also serve to help a child regulate.

The behavior is not willful. We do our youth *harm* when we, as the caring adults, do not see this. Rather than respond with external control as though it *is* willful, parents need to learn to build responses that are *calm and certain,* but not judgmental. When we understand that children who have experienced trauma are not acting in the thinking part of their brains, we can approach them with a new understanding based on a new question: "What's wrong with you?" is replaced with "What *happened* to you?" The changes that happen to a brain that's experienced trauma early are real and lasting, and these children require a different kind of parenting.

"If you have experienced a trauma it can be like having stared directly at the sun. Even after you look away, the glare seems everywhere and prevents you from seeing things clearly. It can keep you from even opening your eyes at all for a while . . . "

–Unknown author

TRAUMA-EFFECTIVE PARENTING: WHERE HEALING HAPPENS

Interpersonal or relational trauma is best healed where the trauma of neglect or abuse occurred, in a relationship. Healthy caregivers who provide predictability, non-judgment, unconditional love, and help with grieving their losses in an open, accepting way, are the best medicine for hurt children. The goal of trauma treatment is to make children feel secure. "You are safe now" is the message they need to hear and feel.

Present Moment Parenting is trauma-effective parenting. It relies on interventions that do not blame, shame, punish, or disconnect a child for normal, natural responses to trauma. Instead, we build bridges with the child to safety, protection, connection, and regulation. Additional trauma comes in the form of disrupted relationships, so sticking with a child and keeping her safe is incredibly important to her healing.

What happens if a child doesn't have consistent, healthy caregiving? Studies show that childhood trauma's effects are 2.5 times worse than wartime PTSD in the military. With neglect, children experience developmental delays. This means that the trauma causes their thinking and processing to be well below their age level. Parents and schools need to be aware of this in helping children who struggle to learn. When kids have consistent caregiving and enlightened teachers, they can thrive!

Trauma is stored in the whole body; not just in the mind or the memory. Trauma is remembered in sensations, smells, and sensory experiences. Some people may assume that because a baby was only two months old when his mother died, he can't remember it and therefore is not affected by it. On the contrary, new studies show that even pre-birth trauma can be detected in the behaviors of children. Furthermore, the field of epigenetics is finding that DNA changes take place in parents when they have been traumatized, and those changes are handed down to their offspring. The effects of trauma are "contagious" through DNA and environment.

Past traumas can be triggered by sensory experiences in the present moment that remind the child of past hurt. Remember that traumatized children are responding today with yesterday's fear. It is not their fault, but rather a brain function issue, designed to help the child survive. The brain mechanism overdoes its job, and simply fails to shut off when the threat no longer exists. This pattern of response can be relearned and healed.

If your own trauma is in the way of being open and accepting, please seek help, so that you can stop the generational cycle of trauma. As the ACE Study indicates that this applies to two-thirds of all US adults, there is no shame in reaching out to heal your own past pain. For some children and most adults, Eye Movement Desensitization and Reprocessing (EMDR) is a highly effective technique. It serves to disconnect the neural pathways that are misaligned in the brain as a result of trauma. Visit www.psychologytoday.com to find a practitioner in your area who uses EMDR. Don't wait, as your child doesn't have time—he is only four or eight or fourteen once, and the sooner you can gain your own self-regulation, the sooner you can heal your child.

WHAT YOU CAN DO AS A HEALING PARENT/CAREGIVER TO SUPPORT THE GROWTH OF YOUR CHILD WITH TRAUMA

1. Bear witness to your child's pain.

2. Let your child know that you see him and hear him, so his brain can be calm and assured of survival.

3. Create space for your child to tell her story while you *listen* (children cannot process when we are talking). Be comfortable with silence.

4. Let your child tell his own story and be the boss of his own grief work. We do not confront "denial" in grief work; the healthy grieving will come naturally when healing happens.

5. Help your child understand that she deserved to get things she did not get when she was younger. Say, "Every baby needs to be cared for, and you deserved to be cared for just like all the others. I am so sorry that didn't happen for you." Let her know this is not her fault and she could do nothing to change it (relieving her of her guilt and shame). To assist your child in processing her losses, try holding her and saying, "If you had been my baby, I would have made sure you had enough good food, clean clothes, and a safe place to live. I would have paid attention to your needs and taken care of you every day, even if you were crying or crabby. I would have let you know I was there for you all the time. If you had been my baby, you would have had everything you needed, when you needed it."

6. Help your child be in touch with his body and places where he holds his trauma, and give him tools to release the trauma: physical exercise, journaling, writing feelings and burning

them, writing to parents who are gone from his life and sending or not sending the letter, crying, throwing rocks into the river, or whatever your child might suggest.

7. Help your child understand her trauma-triggers and trauma-responses.

8. Help your child understand the link between his current behavior and his past experience.

9. Teach skills to help avoid trauma responses by replacing them with relaxation, deep breathing, and other self-regulating skills, in order to respond in the present moment.

10. Use interventions that *connect* instead of *disconnect.*

11. Understand that negative behaviors are not willful, but rather involuntary trauma responses.

12. Understand that punishment exacerbates trauma.

13. Provide a safe, consistent, nurturing place to do your child's grief work.

14. Understand that many behaviors may be developmentally appropriate and normal, healthy responses to grief, loss, and trauma.

15. Help your child feel safe.

16. Provide consistent, repetitive, healing responses.

17. Be a co-regulating partner (sit down and breathe together) and model self-regulation.

18. Value and appreciate your strengths and resilience.

19. Help your child connect with those she's loved and lost and build strong networks of support.

20. Take care of yourself by understanding where your children's behaviors come from, and ways to improve your lives.

21. Nurture yourself spiritually.

22. Practice self-compassion.

23. Refuse to listen to critical comments, knowing that others have no idea what your child has gone through.

24. Forgive your child in the moment of pain-based behaviors.

25. Commit to living in the moment, rather than letting the past or future frighten you or your child.

26. Accept imperfection; look for general improvement.

27. Seek your own supportive resources and healing.

28. Listen with curiosity and openness.

29. Ask for your child's help, opinions, and ideas.

30. Pat yourself on the back for having had a good hour, morning, afternoon, evening, day, week, or month.

31. Learn new ways to approach grief, loss, and trauma.

32. Get vulnerable with your child, appropriately sharing your experiences, feelings, and losses.

33. Be as predictable as possible in routine and connection.

34. Show as much appropriate physical affection as is accepted by your child (hugs, touching while talking, pats on the back, shoulder rubs, or head massage).

35. Observe what your mirror neurons are telling your child.

36. Get help processing your own grief and loss.

37. Express heartfelt, abundant gratitude to your child, to your partner, and to other children.

38. Share funny moments, telling a story about a good moment, or making them happen at home.

39. *Believe it can be better:* hold hope for your child until she can regain her own hopefulness!

40. *Stick with it:* create a permanent bond or connection whenever possible!

"I SEE YOU" LETTERS

Another tool for helping a child with a traumatized brain, or any child who is asking for attention by showing unwanted behavior, is an "I see you" letter. When something is put into writing, it weighs more. The child can read the message without having to hear the adult's voice, which is more effective because adult voices have not proven trustworthy in the past. I encourage caregivers to write the letter in a notebook, so the child can write back if she so chooses, and review the letter at any time. The re-reading can be very healing. When I've encouraged other adults to write this type of letter, they've told me that they've found it later, stashed in a drawer or other safe spot, but never thrown away, which speaks to its significance to the child.

You can write a letter to a child of any age. If she is old enough to read, just leave it on her pillow. If not, write it out and read it slowly, then hand it to her.

If the child is so hurt that listening to you read a letter is too much, try posting notes that say what you see in her all over her room. Use the components below to craft your letter or your notes. The components of the "I See You Letter" are:

1. I see what you've been through (in details that are significant to her, maybe just the things you know she remembers). You may want to add, "And other things, too, that we haven't talked about." This could spark a response where she shares more.

2. In light of your experiences, I realize that none of your recent behavior is your fault. You were just trying to express your pain.

3. I'm sorry I blamed you when I just didn't realize that your behavior was your pain being expressed.

4. Together we'll work on making it better, and here's how: ____

An example:

Dear Isaiah,

I just wanted to tell you what I see when I look at you. I see a kid who has had some very rough experiences. When you were younger, your adults did not do what they needed to do to keep you safe. No child should have this happen, as every child deserves and needs to be kept safe. Your mom left you with people who hurt you, and your dad left without saying why. That must hurt so much. I want you to know that this was never, ever your fault. You were an innocent child.

I see a kid who is sensitive and smart. I see a kid who is amazing at figuring out other people. I so appreciate hearing you express what you know long before others your age can do that. I see a kid with artistic ability, and one who cares deeply for our pets. When I watch you with younger children, I am so impressed with how tender you are.

I realize I have gotten angry with you and yelled when you were upset with me. I now get that you just felt threatened, and you did not mean to hurt my feelings or disrespect me. I'm sorry and I will try very hard not to yell in the future. If I make a mistake and yell (because we all make mistakes), I will apologize and have a do-over, because no one deserves to be yelled at. If you feel like writing back to me in this notebook, that's great. Feel very free to do so. If not, I'm fine with that, too. I'm just happy to be able to use this notebook to say what I want to tell you in writing.

I am so happy you are in my life. Thank you for all the gifts you give me, especially your smile.

Love,

Mom/Dad/Grandma/Grandpa/Other caregiver

I encourage adults not to ask the child if he read the letter, nor to expect him to say he read it and liked it. For a traumatized child, this may be too much vulnerability. But what often happens is that adults notice a softening in their child, a better attitude, more affection, more focus, and more cooperation. That's the goal of writing: to *see the child* clearly, communicate it, allow the amygdala to register that the child is seen and therefore will survive, watch the result in a much more relaxed and relieved child and in an improved relationship. I often describe this process as being "like physics," as predictable as proven science. It's truly remarkable how dramatic the results are! And when you think about it, the seeing is the tool for calming the threat alarm. No wonder the child can now function so much more rationally. The more rational front brain is able to work!

CHAPTER SEVEN

Self-Care, Gratitude, and Self-Compassion in Parenting

Present Moment Parenting may seem daunting. It requires preparation, practice, vigilance, and the mastering of specific skills. It may also seem to require that you forego your own needs to control your intense child. But this need not be the case. In fact, it's vital to pay attention to your own needs on a regular basis in order to successfully implement Present Moment Parenting.

As mentioned in Chapter One, when we travel by air, we hear the phrase, "Place the mask over your own mouth and nose first, and then assist others." This is a powerful metaphor for parenting in today's world. It illustrates the need for self-preservation when facing the enormous task of raising a challenging child. Most of the parents with whom I work have very little concept of self-preservation. They are like hamsters in cages, reacting to whatever comes, with no "big picture" plan for sustaining themselves. What lies beneath this is a belief that they should somehow fill others' cups without filling their own. Or they may just be trying to stay ahead of their child's next impulse. Certainly one can provide for someone else in the short run, while ignoring one's personal needs. But this doesn't work for a sustained period of time without great cost to mental, and often physical, well-being. It's not only all right to set aside "me time," it's vital to your mental health to take a break from this most important and challenging job.

The "Self-Care and Lifestyle Balance Inventory" provided by Headington Institute (www.headington-institute.org) provides an excellent starting point for assessing self-care strengths, as well as areas that could be improved. This tool recognizes that self-care is much more than eating healthy foods and exercising. The tool focuses on our need to laugh and spend time with others, take vacations, and be kind to ourselves when we make a mistake.

Here are some additional ideas for self-care:

1. Make sure the kids go to bed early enough for you to have time to yourself. This is an unbreakable rule, even in the summer. Remember, your mental health requires it.

2. Plan a few hours away each week. Spend time with your partner or friends, get outside, and do something you wouldn't normally do, such as get a massage, have your nails done, take a hike in nature, take photos, or spend time alone in a coffee shop.

3. Once a month, take time for a longer getaway.

4. Arrange for childcare well in advance, so you know your away-time is coming.

5. Journal your parenting experiences: the good, the bad, and the ugly. Forgive yourself for the ugly.

6. Share with other parents online, to avoid feeling alone. Caution: if the parents on a site are mostly negative or cynical, choose another one. You don't need to be fed negative thoughts when you're trying to rejuvenate.

7. Watch shows and movies that make you laugh. Parenting can feel so heavy at times, and humor reminds us to take life more lightly.

GRATITUDE AND ITS CRITICAL ROLE IN PARENTING

It's not uncommon for parents to spend time thinking about the parenting challenges and problems that they're experiencing rather than focusing on what's going well. The field of positive psychology focuses on the scientific study of humans flourishing, and an applied approach to optimal functioning. It has also been defined as "the study of the strengths and virtues that enable individuals, communities, and organizations to thrive." Positive psychology recognizes that some of our happiness is due to external factors, but up to 40 percent comes from how we choose to approach the world. Practicing gratitude is a simple but effective way to increase positive emotions related to parenting.

According to Dr. Robert Emmons, the author of *Thanks!: How the New Science of Gratitude Can Make You Happier,* the act of keeping a gratitude journal and writing brief reflections about moments that make you thankful can increase well-being and life satisfaction.

Recognizing gratitude can be counterintuitive and requires practice to overcome the natural tendency to focus on what is wrong, or not going well. Below are some suggestions for incorporating gratitude practices into your family:

1. At dinnertime have each person write down one thing that he or she saw a family member do well today. Read your gratitude statements out loud to each other.

2. At bedtime, set aside five minutes to reflect on what went well in your day and on things for which you are thankful.

3. Take time to notice the beauty of the world around you while driving yourself to work. Ask your family members to do the same while riding in the car together.

4. Write down things for which you are grateful on slips of paper and put them in your "gratitude jar." This can be done individually or as a family.

5. Write a gratitude letter to someone to whom you feel grateful. Encourage your family members to do the same.

6. Give each family member a gratitude journal and encourage them to spend time every day recording what they appreciate.

7. Use sidewalk chalk to draw pictures or write your gratitude words. This can be done as a family, or siblings could be asked to do this to refocus during times when they're struggling to work together.

8. Put gratitude prompts (see below) in a jar and have each person pick one and share their ideas.

9. End all family meetings with a statement of gratitude.

Gratitude Prompts:

- What am I grateful for being able to do well?
- What happened today that I'm thankful for?
- What is something that I do or see every day that I'm grateful for?
- Who has played an important role in my life?
- I appreciate ________________.
- What opportunities to help others feel good to me?
- What is something beautiful that I appreciate?
- Who made today a better day and how?
- What am I thankful for that I don't have to worry about?
- Whose love makes me grateful?
- What do I get to do every day that I love?

SELF-COMPASSION AND ITS CRITICAL ROLE IN PARENTING

Imagine your best friend failed miserably at her most recent efforts to engage in Present Moment Parenting. Imagine the kind words that you would say to her. Now, imagine it is you who failed. What kind of self-talk would you engage in? Chances are, the words you say to yourself are not nearly as kind as those you would say to your best friend. Self-compassion is about treating ourselves just as well as we would treat our very best friend. A simple concept in theory, but in reality it is anything but. Parenting with self-compassion gives you the opportunity to recognize that you are a human being, human beings are not perfect, and you will make mistakes. There will be times that you, just like your child, will need a do-over. Practicing self-compassion gives your child an opportunity to witness that he, too, can make a mistake, forgive himself, self-correct and move on.

In her book *Self-Compassion: The Proven Power of Being Kind to Yourself*, Dr. Kristin Neff posits that peace of mind does not depend on external circumstances. This is such a counterintuitive thought for parents today, it's a big leap to entertain that it might be true. Doesn't our happiness depend on the health and well-being of our children; our successful interactions with our partner or spouse; our job going well; and positive interactions with friends and relatives?

Dr. Neff points out that we have no control over our immediate emotional reactions to events such as having sick children, having spousal arguments, getting demoted at work, or being estranged from family members. These reactions come from our history, family values, current state of mind, and a wide variety of other sources. But in the present moment, we do have the power to *determine what meaning we assign* to each of the situations. At every turn we are assigning meaning, and it can either be "disaster" or "new issue to be resolved peacefully." Have you ever encountered a teacher or parent who seemed unflappable? She spoke in a quiet voice, seemed to get the children's attention and cooperation, and never seemed frustrated? Did you wonder, and even remark, how does she do it? Self-compassion provides the foundation for her eloquent response.

Dr. Neff outlines three key components to practicing self-compassion:

- **Self-kindness:** Being kind, gentle, and understanding with yourself when you're suffering.

- **Common humanity:** Realizing that you're not alone in your struggles. When we're struggling, we tend to feel especially isolated. We think we're the only ones to experience loss, make mistakes, feel rejected, or fail. But these very struggles are part of our shared experience as humans.

- **Mindfulness:** Observing life as it is, without being judgmental or suppressing your thoughts and feelings.

Suggestions for practicing self-compassion:

1. Treat yourself as kindly as you would treat your very best friend who was having the same experience.

2. Take time to reflect on what you did right and give yourself credit.

3. Remind yourself that you are not alone and that others have had the same or similar experiences.

4. Take time to reflect on the knowledge you have gained from the situation.

5. Remind yourself that you are a human being and there is not one single perfect person in the entire world.

6. Share with other parents online, to avoid feeling alone. Caution: if the parents on a site are mostly negative or cynical, choose another one. You don't need negative thoughts to be fed when you're trying to rejuvenate.

7. Watch movies that make you laugh. Parenting can feel so heavy at times, and humor reminds us to take life more lightly.

MY PROGRESS NOTES:

Obstacles to implementing the ideas in this chapter:

Ways I will overcome the obstacles:

After using the ideas in this chapter, here's my success story:

RESOURCES FOR PARENTS

Dawson, Peg. *Smart but Scattered: The Revolutionary Executive Skills Approach to Helping Kids Reach Their Potential.* New York: Guilford Press, 2009.

Levine, Mel, M.D. *The Myth of Laziness.* New York: Simon and Schuster, 2003. Visit www.allkindsofminds.org for more information.

Neff, Dr. Kristen. *Self-Compassion: The Proven Power of Being Kind to Yourself,* 2011.

Rapp, Doris, MD. *Is This Your Child?* New York: William Morrow and Company, 1991.

Restorative Justice. Visit restorativejustice.org.

Self-Care and Lifestyle Balance Inventory. www.headington-institute.org/files/test_self-care-and-lifestyle-inventory_best_76305.pdf.

Tolle, Eckhart. *The Power of Now.* Novato, CA: New World Library, 1999. Visit www.eckharttolle.com for more information.

Visit www.parentingmojo.com to download the free audio of Tina coaching a parent: "60 Minutes with Parent Coach Tina Feigal."

Also downloadable at www.parentingmojo.com are guides for teachers that correlate with this book: *The Pocket Teacher Coach: Early Childhood* and *The Pocket Teacher Coach: Grades 1-6.*

MAKING HEARTFELT APPRECIATION EFFECTIVE: DAILY REMINDER SLIPS

The positives are where my true power lies. I infuse positivity into my child's heart at every opportunity using "When you _______ I feel _______ because _______" to add intensity.

The positives are where my true power lies. I infuse positivity into my child's heart at every opportunity using "When you _______ I feel _______ because _______" to add intensity.

The positives are where my true power lies. I infuse positivity into my child's heart at every opportunity using "When you _______ I feel _______ because _______" to add intensity.

The positives are where my true power lies. I infuse positivity into my child's heart at every opportunity using "When you _______ I feel _______ because _______" to add intensity.

The positives are where my true power lies. I infuse positivity into my child's heart at every opportunity using "When you _______ I feel _______ because _______" to add intensity.

The positives are where my true power lies. I infuse positivity into my child's heart at every opportunity using "When you _______ I feel _______ because _______" to add intensity.

The positives are where my true power lies. I infuse positivity into my child's heart at every opportunity using "When you _______ I feel _______ because _______" to add intensity.

The positives are where my true power lies. I infuse positivity into my child's heart at every opportunity using "When you _______ I feel _______ because _______" to add intensity.

The positives are where my true power lies. I infuse positivity into my child's heart at every opportunity using "When you _______ I feel _______ because _______" to add intensity.

ABOUT THE AUTHOR

Tina Feigal, MS, Ed. is a passionate parent coach, trainer for professionals, and founder of the Center for the Challenging Child, now a branch of Anu Family Services, Inc. Since 2000, she has developed her coaching and training business, working with people from the US, Canada, New Zealand, England, and Denmark. Tina credits her three sons, Ben, Jordan, and Jacob, for being her main teachers and for inspiring her to help parents and their kids grow the best possible relationships.

Tina has been the parenting coach for Minneapolis-St. Paul's NBC affiliate, KARE 11 TV, offering on-screen parenting tips. She also hosted a parenting web forum at www.kare11.com. Tina offers a regular e-newsletter to thousands of parents nationwide and manages the website www.parentingmojo.com. In addition, she speaks at conferences all over the US to a mix of audiences, addressing bio, foster, and adoptive parents; teachers; social workers; clergy; and childcare providers. She also certifies other professionals as parent coaches using an online ten-month format or a Fast Track version of the class.

Tina believes that putting healing in the hands of adults who love and teach intense and challenging children is the best possible model for improving life with these children. Who better to cause the improvements than the very parents and teachers who raise and teach them? She dedicates her life to seeing parents and teachers become empowered by employing positive techniques that really work!

For more information, visit www.parentingmojo.com.

ABOUT THE CONTRIBUTORS

Amelia Franck Meyer, MS, MSW, APSW, LISW, served for fifteen years as the CEO of Anu Family Services. She is now the CEO of Alia, whose goal is to reform child welfare in the US, creating a well-being transformation so ALL youth in foster care are able to thrive. To learn more, visit www.aliainnovations.org.

Mechele Pitt, MSSW, LCSW, LICSW, has been working in the child welfare field since 1995, and is the current CEO at Anu Family Services. Mechele is passionate about organizational well-being and helping youth and families thrive. To learn more, visit www.anufs.org.

ACKNOWLEDGMENTS

Special thanks go out to our coaching clients at the Center for the Challenging Child and Anu Family Services, without whom we would never have learned the techniques developed for this work so that others could benefit. I also extend sincere thanks to Amelia Franck Meyer and Mechele Pitt, who contributed to Chapters Six and Seven of this book, respectively. And to my fellow coaches, from whom I gain valuable insights, ideas, and methods every day; your work lifts me up, and I am so grateful for your help in building parent coaching as a field. My three sons, their spouses, two grandsons, and granddaughter, who was born during the writing of this book, have inspired my ability to see into the hearts of parents in a way that confounds and also amazes. Without the confounding, the amazement wouldn't be nearly as sweet. My heartfelt appreciation goes out to all of you!